THE TWENTIETH CENTURY WORLD

Josh Brooman

LONGMAN

Contents

So far in the twentieth century, there have been 241 wars around the world. These conflicts have killed some 99 million people. Countless millions have been injured or made homeless. Trillions of pounds have been spent on weapons. The twentieth century has been the most violent in human history.

These wars have led to great changes – in the way we live, in the way we are governed, in our societies and in our work. Some of these changes have been for the better. Some would not have happened without war.

This book is about the two most violent wars of the century, the World Wars of 1914-18 and 1939-45. It describes how they started, what happened in them, and how they changed the lives of people everywhere.

1 The First World War

The First World War in outline

The First World War started on 28 July 1914 and ended on 11 November 1918. People called it the First World War because twenty-eight countries from all parts of the world were involved. Never before had a war spread across the entire globe.

The two sides

The war began when a Serbian gunman murdered the heir to the throne of Austria-Hungary. The Austrian government blamed the Serbs for the killing and declared war on Serbia. Austria's main ally, or supporter, was Germany, so Germany quickly became involved. Later, these two countries were joined by Bulgaria and Turkey. Together, they were known as the Central Powers (see Source 1).

Against them were five countries we call the Allies: the British, French, Belgians, Serbs, and Russians. As the war went on, eighteen more countries joined the Allies. The most important of these was the United States of America. It joined the war in 1917 when both sides were exhausted. Its great power and large army helped the Allies to recover and win the war.

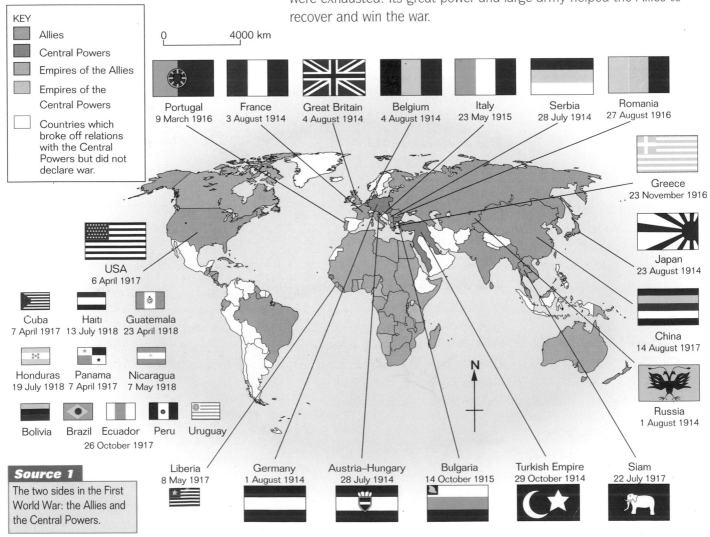

KEY
- Allies
- Central Powers
- Empires of the Allies
- Empires of the Central Powers
- Countries which broke off relations with the Central Powers but did not declare war.

0   4000 km

Portugal 9 March 1916
France 3 August 1914
Great Britain 4 August 1914
Belgium 4 August 1914
Italy 23 May 1915
Serbia 28 July 1914
Romania 27 August 1916
Greece 23 November 1916
Japan 23 August 1914
China 14 August 1917
Russia 1 August 1914

USA 6 April 1917
Cuba 7 April 1917
Haiti 13 July 1918
Guatemala 23 April 1918
Honduras 19 July 1918
Panama 7 April 1917
Nicaragua 7 May 1918
Bolivia
Brazil 26 October 1917
Ecuador
Peru
Uruguay

Liberia 8 May 1917
Germany 1 August 1914
Austria–Hungary 28 July 1914
Bulgaria 14 October 1915
Turkish Empire 29 October 1914
Siam 22 July 1917

Source 1

The two sides in the First World War: the Allies and the Central Powers.

Source 2

Where the First World War was fought, 1914-18.

KEY
→ Allied attack
→ Central Powers' attacks
◆ Major sea battles
⋰ Ships sunk by submarines

Where the war was fought

The war was fought mainly in Europe. The areas where the armies fought were called fronts. The biggest were the Western Front (in Belgium and France in western Europe) and the Eastern Front (in Russia, Austria and Romania in eastern Europe). Outside Europe, fighting took place in the Middle East and Far East. There was also fighting at sea, mostly attacks by submarines on merchant ships.

Total war

Before 1914 most wars were fought on battlefields by armies, or at sea by armed navies. The First World War also involved civilians in a big way. For example, millions of people went hungry, or starved, as each side sank the other's food supply ships. A war which involves everybody, civilians as well as soldiers, is known as a total war.

The human toll

The First World War also differed from previous wars in the number of people who died. An average of 1500 soldiers were killed in action every day of the war. Many thousands of civilians died as enemy armies swept across their lands. Millions more died of hunger or illness. In all, some ten million soldiers and twenty million civilians died as a result of the war.

Questions

1
  a Look at Source 1. Make a list of (a) the Allies, (b) the Central Powers.
  b Which of the two sides was biggest?
  c Which countries fought from the start of the war (July-August 1914) to the end (November 1918)?
  d Which countries joined after the start of the war?

2
  Look at Source 2, then say which of the following statements are true and which are false. If you decide that a statement is false, make up a true statement to replace it.
  a All the fighting took place in Europe: true /false.
  b The largest fighting front was the Eastern Front: true/false.
  c There was fighting in France, Belgium and Britain: true/false.
  d There were very few sea battles during the First World War: true/false
  e Most fighting at sea was done by submarines attacking cargo ships: true/false.

Why did the war become a world war?

The war started in Europe with two countries fighting each other: Serbia and Austria. Within a week, five more countries had joined the conflict. By the time it ended in 1918, twenty-eight countries in six continents were at war. Why did this happen? Why did the war become a *world* war?

Alliances

Look at Source 1. In 1914 the six most powerful countries in Europe were divided into two **alliances**. Germany, Austria-Hungary and Italy were in one. France, Russia and Britain were in the other.

They had formed these alliances for self-protection. The French, for example, wanted protection against Germany, which had made war on France in 1870. The Russians also wanted protection against Germany as they had often been enemies in the past. So the French and Russians agreed to help each other if Germany attacked either of them.

All six countries in the alliances were powerful and well-armed. If a quarrel started between two of them, it was likely to flare up into a war between them all as each asked its partners for help.

This is what happened when Austria and Serbia went to war on 28 July 1914. Serbia asked Russia for help. Although they were not in an alliance, the Serbs and Russians had much in common because many of them were Slavic people. Russia therefore agreed to help Serbia fight Austria. On 29 July the Russian army started to mobilise (that is, to get ready for war).

The alliances go to war

When the German government heard that the Russians were getting ready to fight its ally, Austria, it declared war on Russia. As France was an ally of Russia, the French mobilised their army on the same day.

The German army did not want to fight France and Russia at the same time, because it would have to divide its forces in two. To avoid doing so, it planned to attack France very quickly, beat the French army in six weeks, and then go east to fight Russia. The Germans thought that the Russians would not be ready to fight before then.

So, on 2 August, the German army attacked France at its weakest point, the frontier with Belgium. However, to get to France Germany also had to invade Belgium. Many years before, Britain had promised to protect Belgium against any other country. Britain now honoured its promise. It declared war on Germany on 4 August.

Five members of the two alliances, along with Serbia and Belgium, were now at war.

Empires at war

Three of these countries - Britain, France and Germany - had large empires. Britain, for example, had an empire of fifty-six colonies and dominions scattered all over the world. When Britain declared war on 4 August, all 450 million inhabitants of

Source 1

The European alliances in 1914.

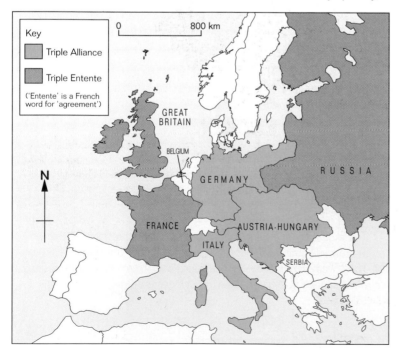

Key
■ Triple Alliance
■ Triple Entente
('Entente' is a French word for 'agreement')

0   800 km

GREAT BRITAIN
BELGIUM
N
GERMANY
RUSSIA
FRANCE
AUSTRIA-HUNGARY
ITALY
SERBIA

these fifty-six possessions were automatically brought into the conflict. Source 3 shows the most important of them.

The same thing happened in the German, French and Belgian empires. Millions of African and Asian people living in German, French and Belgian colonies suddenly found themselves in a state of war.

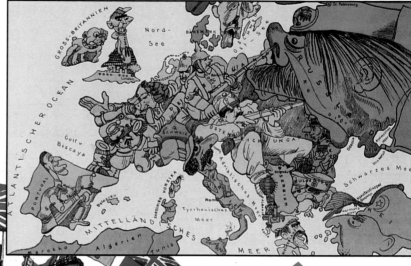

Source 2

A German cartoonist drew this in 1914. It shows the countries of Europe as a tangle of alliances and armies. Find Germany (*Deutschland*) and Austria-Hungary (*Osternach-Ungarn*). Which countries are they attacking? The other countries are looking on, surprised and wondering what to do.

Source 3

This picture postcard was produced as a souvenir for King George the Fifth's coronation in 1911. It shows the flags, held by warriors, of the main colonies and dominions of the British Empire.

Questions

1 Ask your teacher for Copymaster 1. Use the information on these pages to write notes on the copymaster, explaining why countries went to war at each of the following stages: 1. 28-29 July 1914; 2. 1-3 August 1914; 3. 4 August 1914.

2 Look at Source 2 and at your completed copymaster. Which stage in the spread of war does this cartoon help to explain?

3 Look at Source 3. The men holding flags are all very different. What did they have in common?

The war began with two alliances quarrelling in Europe. It spread when they brought their colonies into it. After that, the war continued to spread for many different reasons. Which reasons were the most important?

Japan and Turkey join the war

Next to join the war was Japan (29 August 1914). In 1902 Japan had made an alliance with Britain. It now helped Britain by attacking Germany's colonies in the Far East.

Turkey joined next (29 October 1914). The ruler of Turkey was not sure at first which side to support. Both wanted his support because Turkey could give them valuable help. For example, it could help Germany by seizing the Suez Canal, Britain's vital shipping link with her colonies. In the end, the Turkish ruler joined the Germans when they made him a gift of two powerful warships.

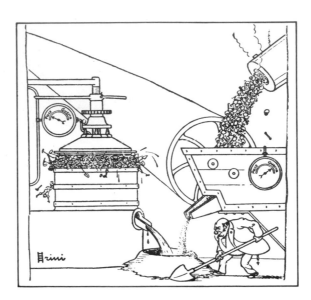

Source 4

This cartoon appeared in an Italian newspaper in 1914, soon after the war started. The machine on the left is squeezing blood from working people. The machine on the right is grinding the bones of dead soldiers. A fat businessman is mixing the blood and bones to make cement. With the cement he will build new factories and new machines to make big profits.

Five late starters

Italy did not join the war in 1914, even though she was an ally of Germany. Source 4 shows one reason why many wanted to keep out of the war. Then, in 1915, Britain and France offered Italy land taken from Austria-Hungary if Italy would join them. Italy accepted the offer and became one of the Allies.

Two other countries joined for similar reasons. Bulgaria joined in 1915 on Germany's side after being promised land taken from Serbia. Romania joined the Allies in 1916 after being offered land captured from Austria-Hungary.

Bulgaria's entry into the war brought Greece into it too. Greece had promised in 1913 to help Serbia if Bulgaria ever attacked it. So, in 1916, the Greeks joined the fighting against Bulgaria.

Portugal was Britain's oldest ally. It had offered to help Britain as soon as the war began. But Britain turned down the offer, thinking the war would be very short. By 1916, the war was still raging and Britain was exhausted. It now gratefully accepted Portugal's help.

The United States and its neighbours

The United States of America (USA) did not want to be involved in a war far away in Europe. From 1914 to 1917 it remained neutral. However, in 1917, German submarines started sinking any ships they found at sea. They were trying to cut off supplies to Britain. Some of the ships they sank were American. Anger at these sinkings led the USA to declare war on Germany in April 1917.

The USA had great influence on many of the other countries in Central and South America. The US President suggested that they too should join the war. Cuba and Panama, where the USA had most influence, joined the day after. Most of the others broke off relations with Germany. The USA also had great influence in an African country, Liberia. It too joined the war on the USA's suggestion on 8 May 1917.

In for the finish: late joiners

As more and more countries joined the Allies, the war began to turn against Germany. When it became clear that the Allies were likely to win, some countries joined in the hope of sharing the rewards of victory.

China had a weak government. Its leaders thought that if they were on the winning side in the war, people both inside and outside China would give them more power and respect. They declared war in August 1917.

Siam (now called Thailand) was surrounded by French and British colonies which had a big say in Siam's affairs. The Siamese government wanted to be free from their influence. Hoping to gain the favour of France and Britain, Siam declared war on Germany.

In Central and South America, more and more countries followed the example of the USA and joined the Allies: Guatemala, Nicaragua, Honduras, Haiti, Costa Rica and Brazil. Four more broke off relations with Germany: Bolivia, Uruguay, Ecuador and Peru.

Source 5

This painting shows US soldiers rescuing French priests and nuns who are being attacked by German soldiers. The artist's aim in painting this imaginary scene was to encourage men to volunteer for service in the army.

Questions

1   Look at Source 4 and read the caption underneath it. How can you tell that the cartoonist did not want Italy to join the war?

2   Look at Source 5. In what ways does the artist try to make American men think they should join the war?

3   Use the information on these pages to finish making notes on your copymaster. The notes will explain why the war spread at each of the following times: 4. August-October 1914; 5. 1915-1916; 6. April-May 1917; 7. 1917-1918.

4   Look at your completed copymaster. At which of stages 1 to 7 did the war spread furthest?

5   Look again at your finished copymaster. It should show five kinds of reasons why countries went to war:

   ● because they were in alliance with another country that went to war
   ● to gain land
   ● because they were influenced by another country
   ● to gain influence in the world
   ● because they were part of an empire.

   a   Make lists of the countries that went to war for each reason.
       (Note: Some countries had more than one reason.)
   b   Which list is longest?
   c   Judging by your completed list, what was the main reason why the war spread to so many countries?

Why did the war last so long?

When the war began, most people thought it would be over in months, perhaps even weeks. 'Over by Christmas' was a common saying in August 1914. People also expected it to be an exciting, glorious war (Source 1). But the war was not over by Christmas. It lasted four years and three months. Why?

War plans fail

Each country had a carefully prepared plan of war in 1914. Germany's plan was to defeat France in six weeks, by invading at high speed through Belgium. Then the German armies would be taken east, to fight Russia. This was called the Schlieffen Plan, after the general who thought it up.

The Schlieffen Plan failed. The Belgian army, helped by a British Expeditionary Force (BEF), put up a strong defence which slowed the German advance. It therefore took the Germans longer than expected to reach France. By the time they were ready to attack Paris, a million French and British troops stood in their way along the River Marne. In the Battle of the Marne, they halted the German advance.

Source 1

An illustration in a German magazine in 1914. It shows British and German soldiers fighting in Belgium. The German soldiers are wearing pointed *pickelhaube* helmets. The British soldiers are wearing bearskins and Glengarry caps.

Stalemate

Both armies then tried to outflank each other. This means that they tried to get round each other's sides. The army which did this would then be able to attack the enemy army from behind. Both armies therefore marched north, hoping to outflank the other before they reached the Channel. Neither side succeeded. All they could do now was dig trenches to stop the other from advancing. The lines of trenches quickly lengthened. By the end of 1914 they stretched all the way from the Channel to Switzerland.

The war plans also failed in eastern Europe. A Russian attack on Germany was halted in two major battles, at Tannenberg and the Masurian Lakes. A massive Austrian attack on Russia was turned back. As in the west, Germans, Austrians and Russians dug trenches to stop the other side from advancing.

On both the Western and Eastern Fronts, the war was therefore now at a stalemate. Millions of soldiers faced each other in trenches which they could not easily capture. Sources 2 and 3 show why it was so difficult to fight trench warfare.

Source 2

An aerial view of British and German trenches in Northern France.

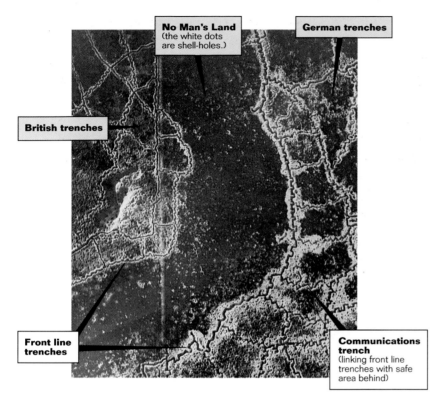

No Man's Land (the white dots are shell-holes.)

German trenches

British trenches

Front line trenches

Communications trench (linking front line trenches with safe area behind)

Source 3

This picture was painted in 1915. It shows German soldiers attacking Canadian soldiers in a trench on the Western Front. Find soldiers firing a machine gun, soldiers throwing hand grenades, barbed wire, and a shell from a big gun exploding.

Questions

1. Look at Source 1. Describe the kinds of fighting going on in the picture.

2. Look at Source 3, then look again at Source 1. How does the fighting in Source 3 differ from the fighting in Source 1?

3. Look at Sources 2 and 3, then make a list of reasons why trench warfare made it difficult for either side to advance.

The war was not 'over by Christmas' in 1914 because a stalemate resulted when each side dug trenches to stop the other from advancing. But why did the stalemate last so long? This section shows some of the reasons by describing two important attempts to break the stalemate.

Failure at Gallipoli, 1915

In 1915 the Allies tried to break the stalemate on the Western Front by attacking in a different place - Turkey. A large army, mainly from Australia, New Zealand and France, invaded Gallipoli in Turkey (Source 5). But the Turks were waiting for them. Thousands of Allied troops were mown down by Turkish machine gun fire as they came ashore. Those who escaped death were unable to advance much further than the beaches. Then, as on the Western Front, both sides dug trenches to stop the other from advancing. A stalemate resulted. It lasted until the Allies withdrew at the end of 1915.

1 Heavy guns bombard the German trenches for 5 days to kill the front line troops, destroy their trenches, and tear gaps in the barbed wire.

3 After the bombardment, British troops climb out of their trenches and form 'waves' of about 1000 men, two metres apart, and advance at walking pace across no-man's land. Further 'waves' follow at 100m intervals.

This diorama (a kind of three-dimensional painting) shows Allied troops landing on a beach in Gallipoli on 25 April 1915.

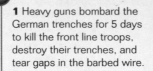

An artist's impression of trench warfare in the Battle of the Somme. This picture was drawn especially for this book. The artist has put together scenes from several different battles to illustrate the main features of the first day of the Battle of the Somme.

Failure on the Somme, 1916

After their failure at Gallipoli, the Allied generals began to think the war could only be won on the Western Front. They pinned their hopes on making massive attacks on the German trenches.

The biggest attack took place in 1916 along the River Somme in France. The Allies planned the attack in great secrecy - or so they thought. For weeks before, German spotter planes watched tens of thousands of soldiers, with guns and ammunition, moving up to the front line. The Germans quickly prepared new defences. They put up extra barbed wire and they dug shelters deep under the ground.

The Battle of the Somme started with a five-day bombardment of the German trenches using big artillery guns. The aim was to destroy the German trenches. But as soon as the bombardment started, the Germans drew back from the front line into their deep shelters. Also, the bombardment failed to destroy the barbed wire in front of the trenches. It simply twisted the wire into a worse tangle than before.

When the bombardment was over, 200,000 British troops advanced towards the German trenches, thinking they had been destroyed. As they advanced, the Germans climbed out of their shelters, bringing machine guns with them. The British were cut down by machine-gun fire. Thousands were trapped in barbed wire. On the first day alone, 20,000 British soldiers were killed.

The British commanders' response was to order more bombardments and more attacks. But the same thing happened each time. By the end of the battle, the British and French had lost 620,000 men, and had advanced only 15 km at the furthest point.

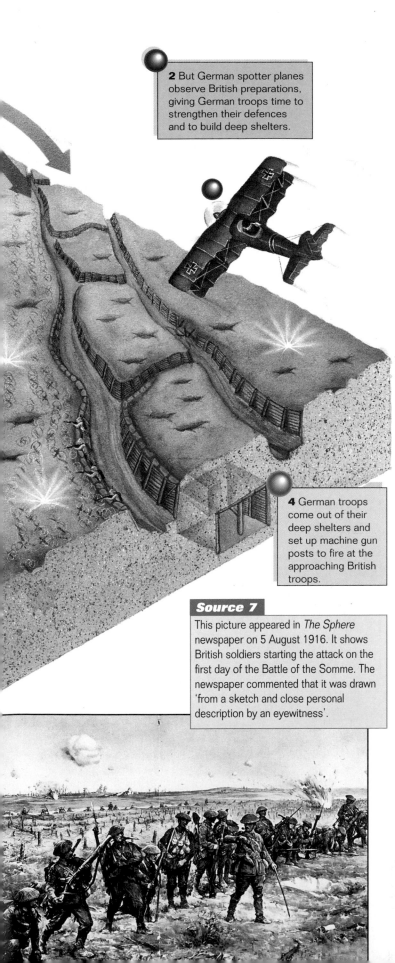

2 But German spotter planes observe British preparations, giving German troops time to strengthen their defences and to build deep shelters.

4 German troops come out of their deep shelters and set up machine gun posts to fire at the approaching British troops.

Source 7

This picture appeared in *The Sphere* newspaper on 5 August 1916. It shows British soldiers starting the attack on the first day of the Battle of the Somme. The newspaper commented that it was drawn 'from a sketch and close personal description by an eyewitness'.

Questions

4 Look at Source 5. What difficulties do you think these soldiers faced in invading Turkey?

5 Look at Source 6. Explain in your own words why the British attack on the Somme on 1 July 1916 failed so badly.

6 Source 6 and 7 are scenes from the Battle of the Somme drawn by artists. Are they likely to be accurate? Explain your answers, using the information in the boxes next to each picture.

7 Using the information and pictures on these pages, explain in your own words why it was difficult to break the stalemate in the First World War.

Britain had the largest, most powerful navy in the world. Of her four enemies, Austria, Bulgaria and Turkey had small, weak navies. Only Germany had a navy of any power. So why couldn't Britain win the war at sea?

Stalemate at sea

Britain and Germany had the largest, most powerful navies in the world. As Britain is an island, it needed a powerful navy to ensure a constant supply of food and materials from overseas. The navy protected the merchant ships which carried these. Britain also needed a large navy to protect its huge empire (see page 7).

So, without a navy, Britain would be powerless. Britain could not, therefore, afford to lose any battles at sea. Winston Churchill, Britain's naval chief, said that the Commander of the Fleet, Admiral Jellicoe, was 'the only man on either side who could lose the war in an afternoon'. For this reason, Admiral Jellicoe did not want to risk battle against the German fleet unless it was unavoidable.

The Germans, however, were unable to take much action either. The German fleet was virtually trapped in its ports by minefields in the Channel and North Sea. For much of the war, the world's two largest fleets - more than 250 warships - lay at anchor in port. Only once did they risk a major battle. This was the Battle of Jutland in the North Sea in 1916. Neither side won a clear victory. Although the Germans lost fewer ships and men, they returned quickly to their ports after the battle and did not venture out again for the rest of the war.

Source 9

A German poster of 1917 shows a submarine commander looking through his periscope, with a merchant ship sinking in the background. The writing says 'The U-boats are out'. (U-boat was short for *Unterseeboot*, meaning underwater boat, or submarine.)

Questions

7 Look at Source 10.

    a   Why did Britain need powerful warships like these?

    b   Britain had by far the most powerful navy in the world. Why then did Britain not quickly attack the German Navy and win the war at sea?

8 Using pages 10-15 for information

    a   make a list of reasons why the First World War did not finish quickly,

    b   explain which of those reasons you think was most important.

Source 10

Battleships of Britain's Grand Fleet, led by Dreadnought battleship HMS *Queen Elizabeth*, patrolling the North Sea in 1916.

War beneath the waves

Beneath the sea, a different sort of naval battle took place. In February 1915 German submarines (U-boats) began sinking ships in the seas around Britain. Their aim was to starve Britain into surrender (Source 9).

To combat the U-boats, the British laid huge minefields in the Channel and the North Sea. The Germans, of course, did all they could to destroy the minefields. As the British minelayers put down the mines, German minesweepers came out to clear them away.

Gradually the Germans gained the upper hand. By early 1917 they were sinking one in every four ships leaving Britain's ports. By the end of April only six weeks' supply of food was left in the entire country. Defeat was avoided when the navy began using a convoy system. Merchant ships sailed in large groups, or convoys, protected by submarine-destroyer ships of the Royal Navy. The number of sinkings dropped to one in a hundred.

The horrors of war

People at the time believed that the First World War was worse than any previous war in history. It was common to hear people say that it must be 'the war that will end war'. Why did they think it was so bad?

The death toll

Source 1 provides one answer. It shows that the death rate in 1914-1918 was much higher than in any previous war. By the time the war was over, more soldiers had died in the fighting than in all previous wars put together. Source 2 shows exactly how many.

Source 1

The average number of soldiers killed each day in ten major wars, 1799-1918.

- Napoleonic War, 1799-1815
- Crimean War, 1854-56
- Prusso-Danish War, 1864
- Prusso-Austrian War, 1866
- American Civil War, 1861-65
- Franco-Prussian War, 1870-71
- Boer War, 1899-1902
- Russo-Japanese War, 1904-05
- Balkan War, 1912-13
- First World War, 1914-18

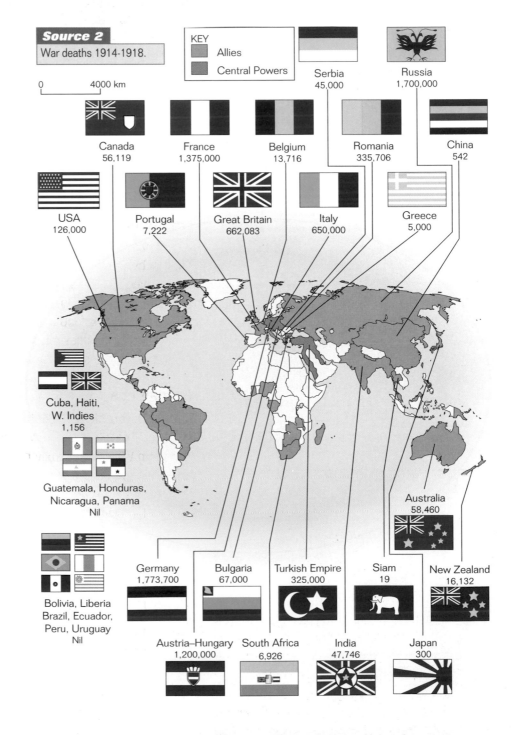

Source 2

War deaths 1914-1918.

KEY
- Allies
- Central Powers

0   4000 km

Serbia 45,000
Russia 1,700,000
Canada 56,119
France 1,375,000
Belgium 13,716
Romania 335,706
China 542
USA 126,000
Portugal 7,222
Great Britain 662,083
Italy 650,000
Greece 5,000
Cuba, Haiti, W. Indies 1,156
Guatemala, Honduras, Nicaragua, Panama Nil
Bolivia, Liberia Brazil, Ecuador, Peru, Uruguay Nil
Germany 1,773,700
Bulgaria 67,000
Turkish Empire 325,000
Siam 19
New Zealand 16,132
Australia 58,460
Austria–Hungary 1,200,000
South Africa 6,926
India 47,746
Japan 300

The war wounded

It wasn't only the number of deaths that shocked people. Equally shocking was the way in which they died. Source 3 shows one of the most common causes of death: shells exploding in trenches. Millions more soldiers were badly wounded. Soldiers could be mutilated by jagged pieces of exploding shells. Poison gas could blind them or ruin their lungs. They could be crippled by bullets. Source 4 shows one of the ways in which soldiers were disabled by their wounds.

Source 3

This photograph of a dead German soldier shows the effect of a shell exploding nearby.

LANDES-KRIEGSFÜRSORGE-AUSSTELLUNG
POZSONY JULI-AUGUST 1917

Source 4

This poster was painted in 1917. It shows a disabled ex-soldier of the Austro-Hungarian army. It was intended to encourage people to give money to the victims of war.

Source 5

The Economic Situation in Germany and Austria-Hungary, a report by the British Foreign Office in 1918.

...the German public is threatened this winter with an almost complete absence of ... electric light, gas, lamp oil and candles. The lack of soap and washing powder makes personal cleanliness impossible and assists the spread of disease. Drugs are difficult to obtain.... For the general public the most pressing question is said to be the provision of warm clothing.... Many of the women have hardly any clothing and are going about clad in a thin blouse and skirt.

Conditions at home

Most previous wars had been fought between armies on battlefields, or at sea by warships. More than any previous war, the First World War involved civilians at home. Airships and aeroplanes were used to bomb enemy cities for the the first time. Both sides used submarines to sink ships taking food and supplies into enemy ports. As a result, food and other supplies ran short in many countries, and had to be rationed. Source 5 shows the effects of this in Germany.

War damage

The war did terrible damage to the land on which it was fought (see Source 6). The worst of the fighting took place in France. An area larger than Wales was totally ruined. Good farm land was churned into useless mud by gunfire. Millions of farm animals disappeared into soldiers' cooking pots. Three quarters of a million homes were destroyed, making two million people homeless.

Source 6

This photograph shows the city of Ypres in Belgium in 1917. Three major battles took place in and around Ypres during the war.

Questions

1. Using the sources and information on these pages, make a list of ways in which the First World War seemed so bad to people at the time.

2. How does this help to explain why people said it must be 'a war to end all war'?

2 Consequences of the First World War

War and revolution (1)

Between 1917 and 1919 there were revolutions in four countries in Europe (see Source 1). In two other countries there were mass protests, strikes and attempted revolutions. Why were there so many revolutions and protests during these years?

The war causes hardship and hunger

Between 1914 and 1918 around twenty million young men served in the armed forces. As you have read, very large numbers of them were killed or wounded. This created a huge shortage of men to work on farms and in factories. The amount of food being grown dropped sharply.

When things are in short supply, the prices usually rise. This is called inflation. In several countries inflation rose rapidly during the war. For people in those countries, food and other goods were not only running short but were also rising in price.

In central Europe, this was made worse by an Allied blockade of enemy ports. Allied submarines made sure that merchant ships could not get into German and Austrian ports. As a result, millions of Europeans were starving by 1918. Source 2 shows how serious the famine was.

Source 1

Revolutions, attempted revolutions, strikes and protests, 1917-1919.

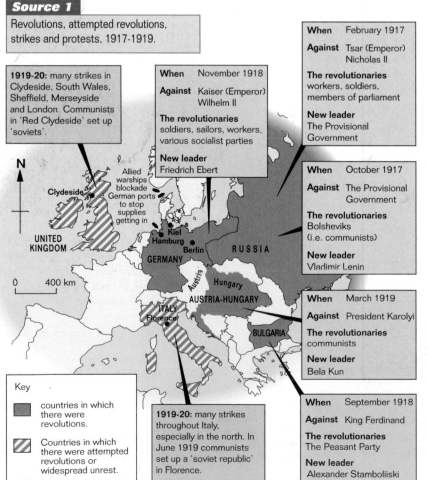

1919-20: many strikes in Clydeside, South Wales, Sheffield, Merseyside and London. Communists in 'Red Clydeside' set up 'soviets'.

When	November 1918
Against	Kaiser (Emperor) Wilhelm II

The revolutionaries soldiers, sailors, workers, various socialist parties

New leader Friedrich Ebert

When	February 1917
Against	Tsar (Emperor) Nicholas II

The revolutionaries workers, soldiers, members of parliament

New leader The Provisional Government

When	October 1917
Against	The Provisional Government

The revolutionaries Bolsheviks (i.e. communists)

New leader Vladimir Lenin

When	March 1919
Against	President Karolyi

The revolutionaries communists

New leader Bela Kun

When	September 1918
Against	King Ferdinand

The revolutionaries The Peasant Party

New leader Alexander Stamboliiski

1919-20: many strikes throughout Italy, especially in the north. In June 1919 communists set up a 'soviet republic' in Florence.

Allied warships blockade German ports to stop supplies getting in

Clydeside

UNITED KINGDOM

N

0   400 km

Kiel
Hamburg
Berlin
GERMANY
RUSSIA
Austria
Hungary
AUSTRIA-HUNGARY
ITALY
Florence
BULGARIA

Key

countries in which there were revolutions.

Countries in which there were attempted revolutions or widespread unrest.

The growing appeal of socialism

In some countries, starving people blamed their governments for the shortages. Many listened to political parties which promised to improve conditions. Some of these were socialist or communist parties which believed in changing society by revolution.

Socialism is a set of ideas about how to organise society. In a socialist society everyone would be equal. There would be no private property. The government would run farms, factories and businesses for the benefit of all people.

Karl Marx and communism

A German thinker, Karl Marx (see Source 3), took these ideas a stage further. He thought that workers in every country would start revolutions against the ruling class - the people who had power and money. These revolutions, Marx thought, would result in a socialist society. But after many years of socialist rule, people would get used to this new way of life. There would be no need for money, laws, or governments. People would live simply, sharing all they had with everyone else. Marx called this way of life 'communism'. He wrote about it in a book called *The Communist Manifesto* in 1848. The most famous sentence of the book says 'Workers of the world unite! You have nothing to lose but your chains!'

Workers and the war

The people who were most attracted by socialism and communism were often factory workers. Before the war, growing numbers of workers had become involved in strikes and disputes over wages and working conditions. Many had joined trade unions.

The war strengthened the trade unions. Workers were as important as soldiers in the war, especially those who made munitions. More workers than ever before joined trade unions to press for better pay and conditions. Source 4 shows what one union was trying to achieve.

Source 2

A British historian describes starvation in central Europe in 1919.

In Vienna children swallowed coal dust to stifle hunger pangs... Sawdust and wood-shavings were mixed with the gruel to bulk it out. In eastern Poland ... post-mortems on hunger victims revealed stomachs filled with sand and half-chewed wood.

David Mitchell, *1919: Red Mirage*, 1970

Source 3

A Russian poster of 1920 shows Karl Marx against a background of factories. It was the factory workers who, he predicted, would organise revolutions.

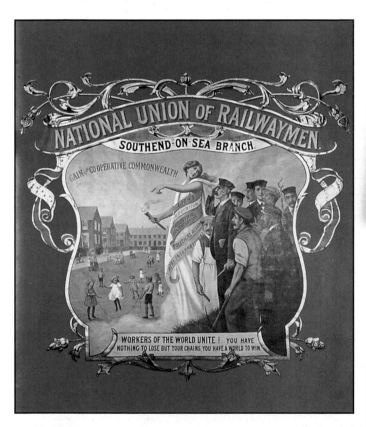

Source 4

This banner was made by members of the National Union of Railwaymen in Southend in 1919. The woman in the middle represents the idea of liberty. She is pointing the way to a better society. The writing underneath is a quotation from *The Communist Manifesto*.

Questions

1 Look at Source 1. What did these revolutions have in common?

2 What does Source 4 tell you about the aims of trade unionists in 1919?

3 Use the Sources and information on these pages to explain why there were revolutions in 1917-19.

War and revolution (2): Russia 1917

The first wartime revolution happened in Russia in February 1917. Angry soldiers and workers forced Russia's emperor to give up his throne. Power changed hands again later the same year. A second revolution in October 1917 brought Communists to power. Why were there *two* revolutions in one year?

Russia before the war

Russia was a poor country. Most Russians were peasants who did not own land, but worked on low pay for harsh landlords. Many of them moved to cities to work in factories, but wages were low, hours were long and housing conditions were bad.

The ruler of Russia was Tsar Nicholas II (see Source 1). Nicholas had enormous power. Although there was a parliament, he usually ignored its advice and made decisions by himself. Growing numbers of people disliked this kind of government.

Russia at war

The First World War made these problems worse. In all, 15.5 million young men were taken into the Russian armies. This halved the number working on farms and in factories. As the output of farms and factories dropped, prices rose. Food and fuel ran short.

Russia's armies suffered many defeats. Soldiers were often badly led and badly equipped. Nearly a million had no rifles. In battle after battle, they were beaten by better led and better fed Germans and Austrians. By 1917 over a million had been killed.

Nicholas tried to improve matters by going to the battle front to lead the armies in person. He left his wife, Alexandra, to run the government. However, Alexandra's key adviser was a faith-healer called Rasputin (see Source 2). Much of the advice he gave her was very bad. Under his influence, she made many poor decisions and appointed second-rate people to government posts. The work of the government ground to a halt.

Source 1

Tsar Nicholas with his son Alexis in 1911. The seven-year-old Alexis had the blood disease haemophilia, which prevents the blood from clotting so that cuts do not heal. There was no cure for haemophilia at this time.

Source 2

Gregory Rasputin (1871-1916) was a monk with faith-healing powers. Unlike any doctor, he was able to stop Alexis's bleeding and ease the pain when he injured himself. However, Rasputin was an alcoholic who behaved outrageously when drunk. He also had many affairs with women at court.

The February Revolution

Nobles loyal to the Tsar murdered Rasputin at the end of 1916. But it was too late to change anything. In February 1917 there were riots in the capital, Petrograd, when bread supplies ran out. Workers on strike against low pay joined the rioters. Soldiers sent to halt the riots also joined in.

In this crisis, twelve members of the parliament set up a committee to take over the work of the government. Nicholas hurried back from the battle front to stop them, but leading army generals told him that the army no longer supported him. Without the army's backing, Nicholas had to resign. He gave up his throne on 2 March 1917.

Source 3

Russian soldiers marching through Moscow in November 1917. Their banner says 'Communism'.

The Provisional Government

The twelve men who took power called themselves the Provisional Government. They intended to make a fairer society and a freer government. But first they intended to win the war. This was a mistake. It meant that the shortages caused by the war continued. And when the Russians were defeated, yet again the Government got the blame.

The Provisional Government had another problem. Many soldiers and workers refused to accept its authority. In cities all over Russia, they set up their own governing councils, called Soviets. Many were led by communists known as Bolsheviks. Their leader, Lenin, summed up their aims in a simple slogan: 'Peace, bread and land'. These three things were what ordinary Russians most wanted: an end to the war; more food; and land of their own. Support for the Bolsheviks grew.

By October 1917 the Bolsheviks were a powerful group. They controlled the Soviet in Petrograd, and they had their own armed force, the Red Guards. Meanwhile, the Provisional Government's grip on Russia was weakening. On 25 October 1917, in a carefully planned plot, Red Guards took control of Petrograd and arrested the Provisional Government.

During the next few weeks, Soviets all over Russia took control of towns and cities. By the end of 1917 most of Russia was in Soviet hands. Russia was now a communist country, and Lenin was its leader.

Questions

1 Many Russians already disliked Tsar Nicholas before 1914. Give at least two reasons why.

2 After 1914 Russians became even more unhappy with Tsar Nicholas. Give at least three reasons why.

3 Use your answers to questions 1 and 2 to explain why Nicholas was overthrown in a revolution in February 1917.

4 Why was there a second revolution only eight months after the first?

War and revolution (3): Germany 1918

In 1918 revolution spread to Germany. Were the causes of revolution in Germany the same as in Russia? And did it have the same results?

The Allied blockade

Throughout the war, Allied warships kept merchant ships out of German ports. As a result of this blockade, there were terrible food shortages throughout Germany.

Food was not the only shortage. As coal ran short, people froze in unheated homes. Lack of soap and washing powder made it impossible to keep clean. When people are starving and dirty, their resistance to disease is low. In summer 1918 400,000 Germans died when a flu virus swept across Europe.

The Kaiser does too little, too late

Source 1 shows that many Germans wanted to change the way Germany was run. Germany's ruler, Kaiser Wilhelm, could have eased their suffering by starting peace talks with the Allies. This would have ended the blockade. He could also have given the people a greater share of power. But he did neither. Public opinion turned against him (see Source 2).

Source 1

Demands of a strikers' meeting, printed in a socialist newspaper on 29 January 1918.

The meeting drew up the following demands: (1) the speedy bringing about of peace... (3) increased supplies of food... (4) the right of assembly and of free discussion in the press and at public meetings... (5) The cancellation of all measures which interfere with the activity of trade unions... (6) the end of military control of industry... (7) the release of all political prisoners... (8) the introduction of the general, equal, direct and secret vote for all men and women over twenty years.

Source 2

This cartoon was drawn in 1918 by a German artist. The man in the centre with bloody hands is Kaiser Wilhelm, the Emperor of Germany. He is in league with war, on the left, and famine, on the right.

Mutiny

In October 1918 Germany's navy chiefs ordered the fleet in Kiel to put to sea for battle. Sailors on two ships refused the order. This was mutiny, and they were arrested. But this made matters worse. The other sailors in Kiel feared that their comrades would be shot for mutiny. They held mass meetings to protest. Workers and soldiers joined them. Led by socialists, they set up a council to run the town.

The mutiny quickly spread inland. All over Germany, soldiers and sailors set up councils to run their towns. Kaiser Wilhelm had lost control of his country (see Source 3). On 9 November Wilhelm abdicated.

A socialist government

Wilhelm's place was taken by Friedrich Ebert, leader of Germany's largest socialist party. Ebert took immediate action to give the people what they wanted. On 11 November, Germany surrendered to the Allies, bringing an end to the war. Next, he ordered improvements in living conditions: a shorter working day, help for the unemployed, increased food supplies. He allowed free speech and arranged elections for a parliament.

Source 4

This poster was made for Ebert's government in January 1919 to make people frightened of the Spartacists. It says 'The Homeland is in danger!' (lines 1-2). 'The tidal wave of Bolshevism threatens our country!' (lines 3-4).

The Spartacist rising

These changes pleased many people, but not all. A group of communists, the Spartacus League, opposed everything that Ebert did. They wanted Germany to be run by the workers' and soldiers' councils, not by a parliament. On 5 January 1919 they tried to seize power by starting another revolution. Armed bands roamed the streets, firing guns and occupying buildings. (See Source 4.)

The Spartacist rising failed. Ebert created a volunteer force of ex-soldiers who hated communists and loved fighting. With extreme violence, they recaptured buildings from the Spartacists and murdered their leaders.

Ebert was now able to hold the elections for parliament which he had promised. In the election his own party, the Social Democrats, won the most votes. On 11 February 1919 the new parliament met in the town of Weimar. Its first action was to appoint Ebert as President of Germany.

Source 3

This photograph was taken in Berlin, capital of Germany, during the revolution of November 1918. It shows soldiers and workers riding around the streets on a stolen lorry. Notice the machine gun on the lorry's roof.

Questions

1 Use Sources 1 and 2 to summarise, in your own words, what many Germans (a) wanted, (b) did not want in 1918.

2 Look at Source 3. What different clues are there in the photograph that Kaiser Wilhelm had lost control of Germany?

3 Look at Source 4.

  a Give another word that means the same as Bolshevism (see page 21).

  b Which country had a Bolshevik government at this time?

  c Judging by the picture and the writing on the poster, what would happen if the tidal wave was not stopped?

4 a Ask your teacher for Copymaster 10 and complete it.

  b Look at your completed copymaster. In what ways were the German and Russian revolutions (i) similar, (ii) different?

'A stab in the back': did Germany really lose the war?

Most Germans wanted peace in 1918. But when their new government surrended to the Allies, many refused to accept that they had been beaten. They said that the government had 'stabbed Germany in the back' (see Source 1). Why did they think this? Let us try to find out by looking at how the war came to an end.

1917: the USA joins and Russia leaves the war

The USA joined the war in April 1917. By the end of the year, 50,000 Americans were arriving in France each week. Soon the Allied armies would outnumber the German army.

Events in Russia gave the Germans a chance to fight back. As you have read, communists came to power in Russia in November 1917. Their first action was to take Russia out of the war. Fighting on the Russian Front ended in March 1918. This meant that huge numbers of German soldiers could be sent to the Western Front. A million Germans arrived there in the spring of 1918.

The German commander, General Ludendorff, decided to use them in a final, all-out offensive on the Western Front. He hoped to win and end the war before many more Americans could arrive.

Allied trenches

1 The offensive begins with a five-hour bombardment of Allied trenches, guns, observation posts and headquarters, followed by a poison gas attack.

2 Then the big guns fire a 'rolling barrage' – i.e. they aim first at the Allied front line, and then move their fire forward at around one km per hour.

The Ludendorff Offensive

The offensive began on 21 March 1918. As Source 2 shows, the Germans used a new method of attack. Outnumbered and confused, the Allied forces climbed out of their trenches and ran. The Germans had broken the stalemate on the Western Front. Now they were marching through open country towards Paris.

However, the German offensive soon ran into difficulties. Too many men went too fast and too far into France. They were soon exhausted and hungry. And their rapid advance meant they could be attacked on three sides by the Allies (see Source 3).

This is exactly what the Allies did. The British, French and American armies made a great counter-attack on 18 July. By the end of August the Germans were back where they had started. In September, they were retreating from their trenches, back towards Germany.

Source 1

This poster of 1924 says 'Who in the World War stabbed the German army in the back?' It goes on to say that it was socialist revolutionaries who betrayed the German army.

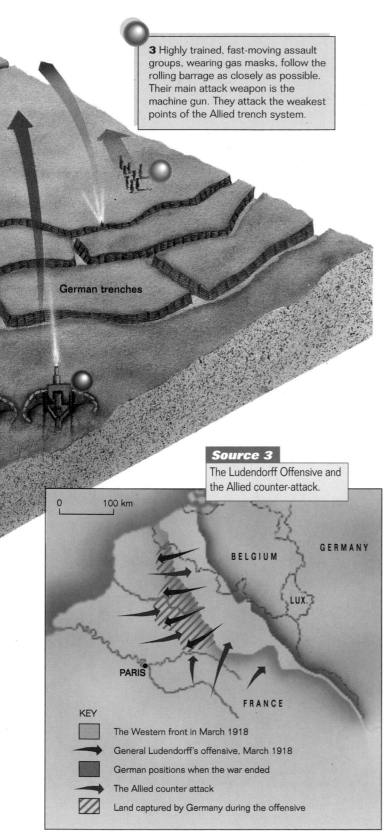

3 Highly trained, fast-moving assault groups, wearing gas masks, follow the rolling barrage as closely as possible. Their main attack weapon is the machine gun. They attack the weakest points of the Allied trench system.

German trenches

Source 3

The Ludendorff Offensive and the Allied counter-attack.

0   100 km

BELGIUM

GERMANY

LUX.

PARIS

FRANCE

KEY

The Western front in March 1918

General Ludendorff's offensive, March 1918

German positions when the war ended

The Allied counter attack

Land captured by Germany during the offensive

Collapse of Germany

Germany itself was now close to collapse. As you have read, thousands of civilians were dying of starvation. A mutiny by sailors triggered a revolution which forced Germany's ruler, Kaiser Wilhelm, to give up his throne. The first action of the new revolutionary government was to sign an armistice, or ceasefire, with the Allies.

November criminals?

The Allies agreed to the Armistice on strict conditions. Germany had to give up all its weapons and warships. Allied troops occupied Germany. The peace treaty which followed six months later was even stricter. It blamed Germany for starting the war, took away huge areas of its land, and made it pay for the damage caused by the fighting.

The Germans were horrified by this. Many said they had been betrayed by the politicians who signed the armistice in November 1918. They called these politicians 'November Criminals' and said that they had 'stabbed Germany in the back' by making peace. The German army, they claimed, could have carried on fighting and could have won.

As you will read later in this book, this was to cause trouble in Germany for many years to come. It even helped to cause a second world war twenty years later. It is therefore important for us to decide whether they were right to say that Germany wasn't really defeated. Decide for yourself after answering the questions below.

Questions

1 a Look at Source 3. How far into Belgium and France had the German army got by March 1918? (Look at the orange line.)

   b How much further into France did the German army get during the Ludendorff Offensive of 1918? (Look at the purple shaded area.)

   c How far into (a) Belgium, and (b) Germany, did the Allied troops get? (Look at the purple line.)

   d How can your answers to questions a, b and c be used to support the idea that Germany was not really defeated in November 1918?

2 Look back to pages 22-23 .

   a Summarise in a few sentences what was happening inside Germany in 1918.

   b Why did Germans feel that (i) they had been stabbed in the back, (ii) they could go on fighting?

3 Using your answers to questions 1 and 2, explain whether you agree that Germany wasn't really defeated in 1918.

The task facing the peacemakers

In January 1919 politicians from the Allied countries met in Paris for a peace conference. Their task was to make peace with the defeated countries. What were they hoping to achieve, and what problems did they face?

Source 1

From *Proposals for Diminishing the Occasion of Future Wars*, a note written by Lord David Cecil, a British government Minister, in Autumn 1916.

It is estimated that the total number of killed and wounded in this war approaches 50 million - more than the population of the British islands .... Total expenditure has been not less than some eight or nine thousand million pounds.... The waste of life, waste of labour and destruction of material has been appalling.... It is surely, therefore, urgent that we should try to think out some plan to lessen the possibility of future war.

© DACS 1995

Source 2

This etching by German artist Otto Dix, created in 1920, is called *War Cripples*. It shows four severely disabled ex-soldiers begging in a street in Germany. Such scenes were not unusual in 1919.

Source 3

A poster issued in 1918 by the British Empire Union warns people not to buy goods from German businessmen after the war.

Anti-war feelings

You have read about the horrors of the First World War (pages 16-17). By 1916 people were saying that it must be the 'war to end all war'. Source 1 shows that some politicians shared this view. The feeling was even stronger at the end of the war. Source 2 shows how a German artist expressed his feelings about the awfulness of the war in 1919. In many countries, therefore, there was public pressure on the peacemakers to make a peace that would last for a long time.

Feelings of revenge

Not everybody shared these anti-war feelings. Millions wanted revenge.

One reason why people felt like this was a belief that enemy soldiers had committed atrocities during the war. People read in their newspapers about German soldiers murdering Belgian babies. Germans heard tales of Belgian nurses gouging out the eyes of wounded German soldiers. And so on. Source 3 shows what some people in Britain felt about German soldiers in 1919.

In fact, none of those things happened. People made up these stories. Even so, there were strong feelings of hatred on either side. Many people said that the peacemakers should take revenge on Germany. In Britain, where a general election was soon to be held, few politicians dared to disagree. Source 4 shows what some of them said about Germany before the election.

National feelings

Some countries which fought in the war contained different nationalities. Britain, for example, contained English, Irish, Scottish and Welsh people. In several countries, the disruption caused by the war encouraged national groups to break free. For example, Hungarian and Czech people broke away from Austria-Hungary. Polish people broke away from Russia. Arab people in the Middle East tried to break away from Turkish rule.

When the war ended, these national groups wanted to remain free. One of the leading peacemakers, the American President, Woodrow Wilson, supported them in this. He said that all nationalities should have the right to live in their own nations and to govern their own affairs. So, one of the peacemakers' tasks was to create new nations for people who had broken free from their rulers. Source 5 shows what Hungarians felt about this.

Source 4

Practically the whole German nation was guilty of the crime of aggressive war conducted by brutal and bestial means.... They must all suffer for it.

> Winston Churchill, part of a speech which he gave in Dundee on 26 November 1918

The Germans, if this government is elected, are going to pay every penny; they are going to be squeezed, as a lemon is squeezed, until the pips squeak.

> Sir Eric Geddes, part of a speech in Cambridge on 9 December 1918

Source 5

A Hungarian poster of 1919 shows a Hungarian revolutionary burying a double-headed eagle in a coffin. The eagle was the symbol of Austria-Hungary. The Hungarians broke away from Austria-Hungary during the war.

Questions

1. What do Sources 1 and 2 tell you about why people wanted an end to all war in 1919?

2. Look carefully at Source 3.
   a. Find seven scenes in the background of the picture. Describe what is happening in as many scenes as you can.
   b. In your own words, explain the message of the poster.
   c. What kinds of people might have agreed with this message in 1918?

3. Look at Source 4.
   a. What does it tell you about British feelings towards Germany in 1918?
   b. Do you think the politicians would have said these things if there had not been an election coming up?

4. a. In your own words, explain why the peacemakers were under pressure to (i) put an end to all war by making a lasting peace, (ii) take revenge against Germany.
   b. Why do you think it might be difficult to do both these things?

BÚCSUZTATÓ
HALOTTI ÉNEK AZ OSZTRÁK-MAGYAR MONARCHIA FELETT
IRTA: KARL KRAUS
FORDITOTTA: SZINI GYULA

KULTURA RT. UTAZÓINTÉZETE BUDAPEST

KÁROLYI KÖNYVTÁR "KULTURA" KIADÁSA

Was the peace settlement unfair on Germany?

The peacemakers drew up peace treaties with each defeated country. These treaties took land and money from them, and reduced their armed forces. The defeated countries complained that the treaties were unfair. The Germans complained loudest of all. What did the settlement do to Germany, and was it really as unfair as the Germans said?

The Armistice

You have read that the Germans signed an armistice with the Allies. This was an agreement to stop fighting while a peace treaty was drawn up. When they signed it, the Germans believed that the treaty would be based on a fourteen point peace plan drawn up by President Wilson of the USA. Wilson's plan contained fair and democratic ideas, so the Germans assumed that the treaty would also be fair and democratic.

Source 1

The Paris Peace Settlement of 1919.

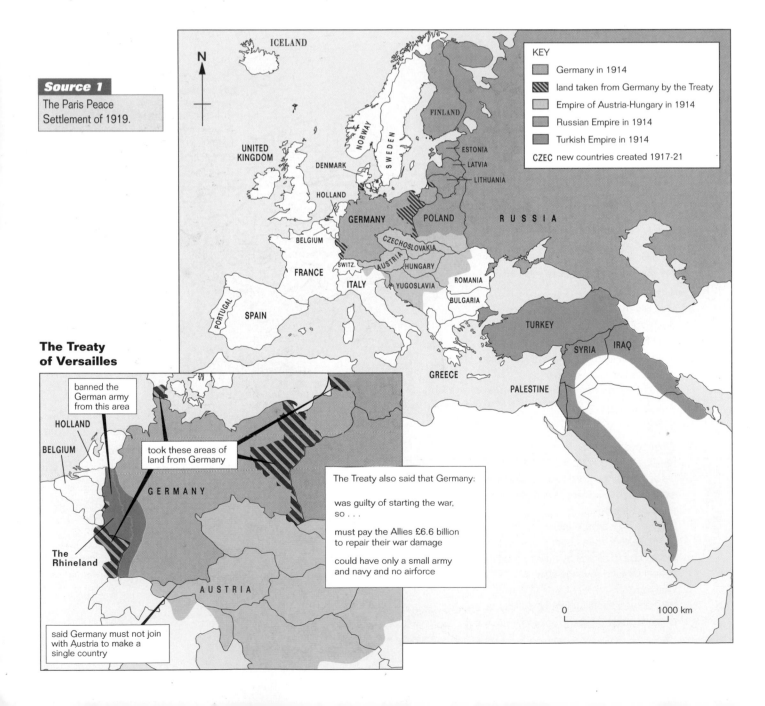

KEY

Germany in 1914

land taken from Germany by the Treaty

Empire of Austria-Hungary in 1914

Russian Empire in 1914

Turkish Empire in 1914

CZEC new countries created 1917-21

The Treaty of Versailles

banned the German army from this area

took these areas of land from Germany

The Rhineland

The Treaty also said that Germany:

was guilty of starting the war, so . . .

must pay the Allies £6.6 billion to repair their war damage

could have only a small army and navy and no airforce

said Germany must not join with Austria to make a single country

0   1000 km

The Treaty of Versailles

The peacemakers spent four months talking about the treaty. The Germans were not included in the talks. They did not see the treaty until the Allies finished writing it. When they did see it, they were horrified. It was much harsher than Wilson had led them to expect.

Only the first part of the treaty was based on Wilson's ideas. This created an international organisation called the League of Nations. Its job was to keep the peace between nations and to get them to work together.

The rest of the treaty was designed to weaken Germany so much that it could never fight a war again. It took away 70,000 square kilometres of land from Germany and gave it to five neighbouring countries. (See Source 1.) It also took away all Germany's colonies.

It slashed the size of the German army and navy, and scrapped its air force. Allied armies were to occupy all of Germany west of the River Rhine. German forces were not allowed closer than 50 kilometres to the Rhine.

Finally, the Treaty blamed Germany for starting the war and said it must pay the Allies for the cost of repairing war damage. The amount was later fixed at £6.6 billion - equivalent to about £112 billion in today's prices.

Reactions to the Treaty

When the German people found out what the Treaty said, they reacted angrily. There were mass demonstrations all over the country. The cartoon below (Source 2) summed up many people's feelings about the Treaty.

The German government protested to the Allies, but they could not persuade them to change the treaty. The Allies gave the Germans five days in which to sign it. If they did not sign, the Allies would invade Germany. Reluctantly, the German parliament voted to accept the treaty.

Source 2

A cartoon from a German magazine of 1919 shows Germany as a man being tortured in a dungeon. While the Allied leaders in the background look on, two masked torturers rip out the man's intestines.

Questions

1 Look at Source 1 and the information in the text.
   a   What were the main changes that the peace settlement made to the countries beaten in the war?
   b   Which aspects of the Treaty do you think Germans disliked?

2 Source 2 compares the Allied peacemakers with torturers ripping out a man's insides.
   a   Judging by Source 1, why do you think the cartoonist portrayed the peacemakers in this way?
   b   Do you think it was a fair comparison?

3 a   In your own words explain why many Germans thought the Treaty was unfair.
   b   Do you agree or disagree with the view that it was unfair? Explain your answer.

Depth Study

3 British women at war

Look at the woman on the right in the photograph below. Her name was Mairi Chisholm. She was eighteen when the First World War began.

Mairi Chisholm was the oldest daughter in a noble Scottish family. Like many other young women, she wanted to help Britain fight the war. Against her mother's wishes, she rode to London on her motorbike, and became a motorbike messenger in the Women's Emergency Corps.

Mairi impressed everyone with her riding skills. After only a few weeks, she was asked to become an ambulance driver in Belgium. There, she was put under the charge of a nurse called Elsie Knocker. She is on the left in the photograph. Together they set up a field hospital in a cellar, only metres behind the trenches, in a village called Pervyse. In this cellar they treated soldiers who were too badly wounded to be moved to safety.

It was dangerous, hard and unpleasant work, but Mairi and Elsie soon became famous for it. Officers came from far and wide to visit them and to praise their work. In 1915 the King of Belgium decorated them with medals.

In 1916, Elsie married one of their patients, a Belgian pilot from one of Belgium's oldest families. She thus became a baroness - the Baroness Elsie de T'Serclaes.

Mairi and Elsie remained at Pervyse until, in 1918, they were badly wounded by mustard gas in a German gas attack. They were in hospital for the rest of the war.

So, for the two 'women of Pervyse', the war brought excitement, danger, fame, and then serious injury. War changed their lives greatly. How typical were they? Did every British woman who helped the war effort experience such great changes? Let us begin thinking about that question by looking at British women's lives before the war.

Source 1

Mairi Chisholm (right) and Baroness Elsie de T'Serclaes (left) photographed in 1917 outside the field hospital they set up in Pervyse in Belgium.

Women before the war

Women as wives and mothers

Women in the 1900s spent much of their time working at home. They brought up their children, and provided them with much of their teaching. They fed, clothed, and cared for their families, and nursed them when they were ill. They cleaned and maintained the house. They managed the family's money. Often, they made the key decisions about the family's life. Sources 1 and 2 help us to understand the importance of this work.

This photograph was taken in 1910. The woman is giving her family tea in the kitchen. All the cooking was done on the coal-fired range in the fireplace.

From *At the Works*, a survey of people's work in Middlesborough in 1907. Lady Bell, the author, visited more than a thousand people in her homes when making her survey.

The key to the condition of the workman and his family...is...the woman who manages his house; into her hands...the future of her husband is committed, the burden of family life is thrust.... The pivot of the whole situation is the woman, the wife of the workman and the mother of his children.

Questions

1 a Look carefully at Source 1. What does it tell you about the different kinds of work that this woman did in the home? (You should be able to think of at least three kinds of work.)

    b Do you think this woman's work was easier or harder than work in the home today? Explain your answer.

2 Read Source 2. Why did Lady Bell think that a woman's work in the home was important?

Women in paid work

Just over half of all single women, and one in seven married women, worked outside the home to make money. Source 3 shows the most common kinds of work that they did.

Women in paid work were not treated in the same way as male workers. Most employers thought that 'a woman's place is in the home', while men were the main breadwinners. Sources 4 and 5 show some of the ways in which women were affected by this attitude.

How women were expected to behave

Most people were brought up to think that a woman's main role in life was to support her husband and her home. A woman was therefore expected to spend most of her time in the home. Apart from going out to shop or to visit neighbours, a woman rarely went out of the house. When she did, it was expected that a man or a female companion should walk with her.

Women were expected to act in a more restrained way than men. For example, while working men commonly spat, swore, smoked or drank alcohol in public, it was rare for women to do any of these things. There were also strict unwritten rules about how a woman should dress. Women always wore skirts or dresses, never trousers, and these were always ankle-length so that their legs could not be seen. Well-dressed women often wore tight girdles, and large hats. (See Sources 6 and 7.)

Women's rights

Women did not have the same rights as men. In particular, they did not have the same voting rights. Women over 30 who paid rates (a local council tax) could vote in elections for their local council. But no women could vote in a general election for Parliament. Around eight million men had this right.

Source 3

The ten most common paid occupations of males and females aged ten years and upwards, 1911 (in thousands).

	Males	Females
Domestic service (e.g. maids, cooks, butlers)	456	2127
Metal manufacture (e.g. shipbuilders, steel-workers)	1795	128
Transport (e.g. train drivers, dock workers)	1571	38
Textiles (e.g. cotton spinners, weavers)	639	870
Agriculture (e.g. farmers, foresters, shepherds)	1436	60
Clothing (e.g. dress-makers, hatters, shoe-makers)	432	825
Mines and quarries (e.g. coalminers, slate quarriers)	1202	8
Building (e.g. bricklayers, carpenters, plumbers)	1140	5
Food and drink (e.g. bakers, brewers, publicans)	806	308
Commercial (e.g. clerks, typists)	739	157

Source 4

From a survey by C V Butler, *Domestic Service. An Enquiry by the Women's Industrial Council*, 1916.

I am a cook and have been in service twenty years.... I rise early and am at work all day long. First thing in the morning I have to light four or five fires and clean the steps before breakfast, besides cleaning the breakfast room, cooking breakfast, cleaning boots, fetching up hot water and tea to those upstairs. I get out for but a few hours once a week.

Source 5

From a survey by Edward Cadbury, Cecile Matheson and George Shann, *Women's Work and Wages. A Phase of life in an industrial city*, 1906.

In the enquiry as to wages we found that whenever women had replaced men the former always received a much lower wage. This wage had nothing to do with the skill or intelligence required by the work but was of a fixed level - about 10 shillings to 12 shillings per week. The wage that the man previously received was no guide to what the women would get, though in general we may say that a woman would get from one-third to one-half the wages of a man.

Source 6

This is an illustration from a women's fashion magazine in November 1907. It shows a 'day dress' - that is, a dress suitable for everyday wear, as opposed to an evening dress which was more formal and elaborate.

Source 7

An advertisement from *The Queen* magazine in 1905. A corset was made from stiffened, rigid cloth to make a woman look thinner than she really was.

Questions

3 Look at Source 3.

 a Imagine visiting the following places of work in 1911: a cotton mill, a farm, a dress-maker's workshop, an office. In which one would you have been (i) most likely, (ii) least likely to have seen women at work?

 b What was the most common occupation for women in 1911?

 c What does Source 4 tell you about this occupation?

4 What do Sources 4 and 5 tell us about women in paid work?

5 Look at Sources 6 and 7.

 a How would wearing clothes like these have affected a woman's actions?

 b What do these clothes tell us about people's attitudes towards women in the 1900s?

6 Prepare a short talk or a wall display showing the main features of women's lives in the 1900s.

What did women do in the war?

Women were involved in the war in many different ways. What did they do in the war, and how did this affect them?

Women workers

At first, the war put many women workers out of their jobs. For example, fishery workers were put out of work when trawlers stopped fishing in waters patrolled by German warships. This soon changed. As the army grew in size, women found work making equipment for soldiers. During 1915, many women also took on the work of husbands, brothers or fathers who joined the army. They did all kinds of work, for example, they became clerks, bus conductors, window cleaners, and coal carriers (see Source 1).

The army needed huge amounts of weapons and ammunition, especially shells. For example, on a single day in 1918, British big guns fired 943,847 shells at the German trenches. As more and more men joined the army, women took the place of male workers in the munitions factories. They made guns, shells, grenades, bullets, and every other kind of weapon (see Source 2).

Women in uniform

Factory work wasn't the only war work which women did. Over 100,000 worked as nurses. Most belonged to units called Voluntary Aid Detachments, and were known as VADs. Thousands of women also joined organisations to help the government deal with wartime problems. For example, the Women's Volunteer Reserve did such things as finding homes for refugees, running air-raid shelters, and working as motorbike messengers.

In 1917 the army set up a Women's Army Auxiliary Corps (WAAC). Its members did non-combat jobs normally done by soldiers, freeing the soldiers to fight. By 1918 there were 40,000 Waacs working as, for example, clerks, drivers and telephonists. A Women's Royal Naval Service (WRNS) and a Women's Royal Air Force (WRAF) did similar work for the navy and the air force (Source 3).

The biggest uniformed organisation for women was the Women's Land Army. There were 113,000 'Land Girls' who worked on farms to replace male farmworkers who joined the army. Their work was vital to the war effort because German submarines were preventing ships from bringing food into Britain from overseas.

Pay and conditions

During the war women's pay more than doubled. Average wages rose from eleven shillings (55 pence) a week to 25 shillings (£1.25) in 1919. Munitions workers could earn even more than this (see Source 5).

The work that women did could not be done in the kind of clothes they wore before the war. Skirts became much shorter. Many women wore trousers instead of skirts. Corsets went out of fashion and dresses became looser. Hair styles also changed, as long hair could be a danger when working with machinery. Sources 1–3 show some of the ways in which women dressed during the war.

Working conditions were often very bad. Hours were long, and shift work could be awkward for mothers with small children. For munitions workers especially, working conditions were dangerous. Women who worked with high-explosive TNT were nicknamed canaries because the explosive chemicals made their hair and skin turn yellow. Accidents often happened (Source 7).

Source 4

The number of women in paid employment, 1914-1918

Occupation	Estimated number of females employed in		Numbers of men directly replaced by women
	July 1914	January 1918	
Industries	2,175,500	2,708,500	503,000
Government establishments	2,000	209,500	197,000
Gas water and electricity	600	5,100	4,000
Agriculture	80,000	74,000	31,000
Transport	17,000	93,000	78,000
Tramways	1,200	18,200	16,000
Finance and banking	9,500	70,500	57,000
Commerce	496,000	839,000	342,000
Professions	50,500	100,500	22,000
Hotels, public-houses cinemas, theatres, &c	181,000	207,000	45,000
Civil Service, Post office	60,500	108,000	53,000
Other Civil Service	5,000	81,500	70,000
Other local authority services	196,200	226,200	24,000
Total	3,275,000	4,741,000	1,442,000

Source 5

From a letter written by Mrs H A Felstead to the Imperial War Museum on 27 January 1976.

I was in domestic service and hated every minute of it when war broke out, earning £2 a month working from 6.00 am to 9.00 pm. So when the need came for women war workers my chance came to 'out'. I started on hand cutting shell fuses.... We worked twelve hours a day.... As for wages I thought I was very well off earning £5 a week.

Source 6

From the memoirs, written in 1978, of a munitions worker called Peggy Hamilton. Peggy's wage of nine pence an hour in 1918 was equivalent to 61 pence today.

We women started at sixpence (2.5 pence) an hour and by 1918 had reached the giddy height of nine pence an hour, while the men were paid 1s 3d.... We did resent the fact that whatever our output or whatever skills we learned or performed, we always received only just over half what the men did for doing exactly the same job.

Source 7

From a tape-recording of 1976, in which a munitions worker recalled her wartime experiences.

A girl that went out left all the powder in the oven and Cissie Peters went on night duty. She opened the oven door and it blew both her eyes out.... There were crowds of accidents but it was all hushed up. I remember one night about six ambulances came along but they wouldn't tell us because they'd be afraid people would leave.

Questions

1 Use the text and Sources 1 to 7 to:
   a list at least four ways in which women helped in the war effort;
   b describe at least four ways in which women's lives were changed by doing these things.
2 Judging by Sources 1 to 7, explain which of these changes you think were
   a changes that improved women's lives;
   b changes for the worse.

The war and women's rights

In 1918 many women gained the right to vote in general elections. Women had been campaigning for this right for over fifty years. Why did they win it during a war?

Women's voting rights in 1900

Before the war, women had very few voting rights. They were not allowed to vote in general elections. They could vote in local elections but only if they were householders or the wives of householders. More and more women saw this as unfair. By 1900 some 50,000 belonged to the National Union of Women's Suffrage Societies. The aim of these suffragists was to gain the same voting rights as men. They gave out leaflets, ran newspapers, held meetings and organised petitions. Source 1 is one of their posters.

The Suffragettes

By 1900 the suffragists had been campaigning for forty years. They still did not have the vote. Some women felt that a more active campaign was needed. In 1903 Mrs Emmeline Pankhurst, with her daughters Christabel, Sylvia and Adela, formed a Women's Social and Political Union to put pressure on the government. They did so by using militant protests, for example by wrecking political meetings. Press reports of such protests made them the best known campaigners for women's votes. Newspapers called them 'suffragettes'.

Militant protests

The government refused to give in to the suffragettes' protests, so they stepped up their actions. For example, they chained themselves to railings in public places, and smashed windows in public offices.

Source 1

This poster was designed by a suffragist in 1908. It made the point that the only men who did not have the right to vote were convicts and lunatics, while a woman could not vote even if she was a highly educated graduate.

A large number of suffragettes were sent to prison for these militant protests. However, many jailed suffragettes went on hunger strike. They hoped to get so much publicity that the government would back down. The government responded by ordering that hunger strikers must be fed by force. But stories of brutal force-feeding gave the suffragettes great public sympathy. Source 2 shows one way in which the public got to know about force-feeding.

In 1910 the suffragettes began a new campaign of violence. For example, they cut telephone wires, smashed shop windows, and set fire to post boxes. They thought the government would give in simply to halt the violence.

The First World War

When the war began in 1914, the suffragettes halted their campaign so that they could support the war effort. The government released over 1000 suffragettes from prison. However, the issue of votes for women did not go away as a result. A new problem about voting now arose. The problem was that a general election would have to be held when the war ended. But, because Britain was at war, the old method of drawing up lists of voters could not be used. Men could only vote if they had lived at the same address for a year. Several million men were now away from home, serving in the armed forces. One man in five would not be on the voting list.

In 1916, therefore, the government made plans for a new list of voters. The suffragettes demanded that any new list should include both women and men. By this time, more than a million women were doing war work. This changed public opinion. Many people felt that women had 'earned' the right to vote.

Women get the vote

In 1918, Parliament finally changed the voting laws. The Representation of the People Act gave the vote to all men over 21 and to women over 30 who were householders or married to householders. Ten years later, in 1928, another Act reduced the voting age for women to 21, and scrapped the rule that women must be householders or the wives of householders. Women thus, for the first time, had the same political rights as men.

Source 3

Adapted from E.Sylvia Pankhurst's autobiography, *The Suffragette Movement*, 1931.

> Undoubtedly the large part taken by women during the war was a tremendous argument for giving them the vote. Yet ... militancy ... was a much stronger factor.

Source 4

Millicent Fawcett, *Progress of the Woman's Movement in the United Kingdom*, 1922.

> I do not believe we would have won the vote just when we did, except for the fact that it was necessary ... to prevent many millions of men who had served their country from losing the vote.

Source 2

This poster, designed by a suffragette artist in 1910, is an impression, based on eye-witness accounts, of how hunger-strikers were force-fed in prison. Prison warders held down the striker while a doctor inserted a tube through the nose and throat, and poured liquid food into the stomach.

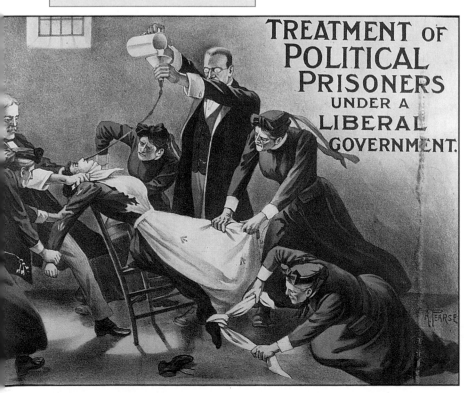

TREATMENT OF POLITICAL PRISONERS UNDER A LIBERAL GOVERNMENT.

Questions

1 Look at Sources 1 and 2. Which poster do you think would have created most sympathy for the idea of votes for women? Explain your answer.

2 Look at Source 3.
   a What reasons does Sylvia Pankhurst give for women getting the vote?
   b What was 'the large part taken by women during the war'? Why was this an argument for giving them the vote?
   c What was 'militancy'? Do you think militancy would have got women the vote if there had not been a war? Explain your answer.

3 What does Mrs Fawcett (Source 4) say was the reason why women got the vote?

4 Which of the explanations in Sources 3 and 4 do you agree with? Explain your answer.

Women after the war

You have read that women's lives were changed by their involvement in the First World War. How far-reaching were these changes? And were they changes for the better?

Women workers

When the war ended in 1918, four million British servicemen started returning to the homes and jobs they had left behind.

Women had been allowed to take over many men's jobs for as long as the war lasted. Now that it was over, they were expected to give their jobs to returning servicemen. Even in factories that had not existed before the war, many women were made to hand in their notice. Within months of the end of the war, hundreds of thousands of women were out of work.

Many of these women did not want to go back into traditional 'women's work' when they lost their jobs. Domestic service was especially unpopular. Many stayed on the dole rather than go into domestic service. These women faced fierce criticism. Newspapers called them parasites and scroungers. The government cut unemployment pay to force them back to work. As a result, most women went back to the kind of work they had been doing before the war. Source 1 shows the ten most common women's occupations in 1921.

Source 1

The ten largest paid occupations of women in 1921.

Domestic service (e.g. maids, cooks)	1,845,000
Textiles (e.g. cotton spinners, weavers)	701,000
General and unclassified (e.g. shop assistants, factory hands)	688,000
Clothing (e.g. dress makers, hatters, shoe-makers)	602,000
Commercial (e.g. clerks, typists, secretaries)	587,000
Professional (e.g. lawyers, doctors, teachers)	441,000
Metals and machines (e.g. clock-makers, equipment makers)	175,000
Food and drink (e.g. bakers, confectioners, brewers)	123,000
Paper, printing, books (e.g. book binders, stationers)	121,000
Agriculture (e.g. farm workers, gardeners)	90,000

Women's rights

Although many women lost their jobs at the end of the war, some did benefit from a new law about work made in 1919. It said that being female or being married could not stop a person from getting a job in the government, the law or any other profession. This meant that women could now enter any job in the civil service, the law and local government. Also in 1919, a State Register of Nurses was set up, and nursing was recognised for the first time as a profession.

You have read that women over 30 gained the right to vote in general elections. Also in 1918 they gained the right to stand for election as a Member of Parliament. Source 2 shows the number of women who became MPs.

As well as these political rights, women gained some important legal rights in the next few years. For example, the divorce laws were changed so that a wife could divorce her husband for adultery and no other reason. Before, she had to prove that her husband had also deserted her or

Source 2

Women candidates in elections for Parliament, 1918-1929.

Year	Number of women elected as MPs	Total number of MPs
1918	1	707
1922	2	615
1923	8	615
1924	4	615
1929	14	615

been cruel to her. A woman could also divorce her husband for drunkenness or for forcing her to have sex. Neither of these had been grounds for divorce before.

Women in society

During the war, women got used to doing things that were frowned upon before, such as smoking, going out alone, and wearing trousers or shorter dresses. This trend continued after the war. Hemlines rose, and by 1926 were near the knee. Smoking became fashionable. Young women went out with men without a companion. Source 4 suggests that some women's lives were much more free in the 1920s than they had been before the war.

Source 3

This photograph shows supporters of Christabel Pankhurst, a candidate in the 1918 general election, campaigning for votes in London.

Source 4

This picture appeared on a magazine cover in 1926. Before the war, it would have been unthinkable for young women to appear in public like this.

Questions

1 Look at Source 1, then look at Source 3 on page 32.

   a In which occupations were there more women in 1921 than 1911?

   b In which occupations were there fewer women in 1921?

   c In which occupations did the biggest changes take place?

   d In general, does Source 1 show that women's work changed a great deal between 1911 and 1921? Explain your answer.

2 a What change in women's rights is shown in Source 3?

   b Look at Source 2. Explain how important you think this change was.

3 Look at Source 4.

   a What aspects of this picture show that women were more free in 1926 than they had been before the war?

   b Do you think the picture gives an accurate impression of women's freedom in 1926? What doesn't it show?

4 The world between wars 1919-1939

The 1920s: a time of hope?

The aim of the peacemakers in 1919 was to make sure there would never again be a world war. Over the next ten years, world leaders tried to ensure that the peace would last. By 1929 their efforts seemed to be working. Many people believed that the world had entered a new era of peace between nations. Why were the 1920s a time of such high hopes?

The League of Nations

As you have read, the peacemakers created a new world organisation called the League of Nations. The League's aim was to keep the peace between nations and to get them to work together on solving international problems.

In its first ten years, the League achieved a great deal. It took steps to settle ten quarrels between its members (see Source 1). It also tried to solve several international problems. For example, it set up a World Health Organisation to try to wipe out diseases like leprosy and smallpox. Other organisations tried to improve people's working conditions, to stop drug smuggling, and to help homeless refugees. It also had a Court of International Justice to try legal disputes between countries. Source 2 shows the main organs of the League and gives examples of their work.

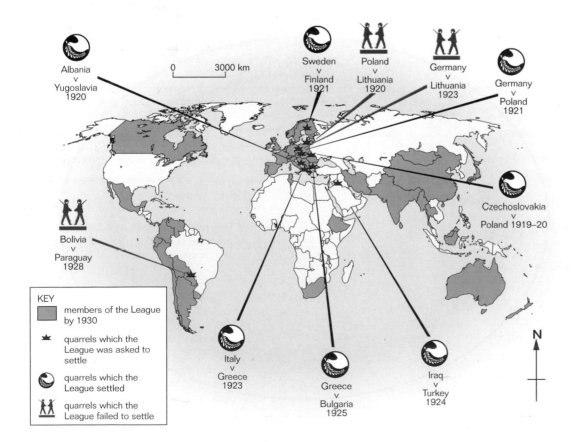

KEY
- members of the League by 1930
- ★ quarrels which the League was asked to settle
- quarrels which the League settled
- quarrels which the League failed to settle

Albania v Yugoslavia 1920

Sweden v Finland 1921

Poland v Lithuania 1920

Germany v Lithuania 1923

Germany v Poland 1921

Czechoslovakia v Poland 1919–20

Bolivia v Paraguay 1928

Italy v Greece 1923

Greece v Bulgaria 1925

Iraq v Turkey 1924

0 3000 km

N

Source 1

Disputes between countries which the League was asked to settle during its first ten years.

Source 2

International organisations run by the League of Nations in the 1920s. In the centre is the Palace of the League of Nations in Geneva, the League's headquarters from 1937 onwards.

The Assembly

A sort of world parliament. Each country had one vote, The Assembly discussed all kinds of world problems and suggested solutions.

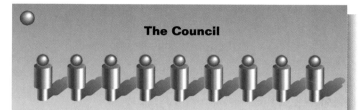

The Council

A small decision-making body. It had five permanent members in 1929 (Britain, France, Germany, Italy and Japan) and four temporary members. It met whenever a dispute between countries flared up. Its main power to stop one country attacking another was to ask all members of the League not to trade with that country.

Court of International Justice

This was based at the Hague in Holland. It had fifteen judges from different countries. It dealt with legal disputes between countries.

Commissions of the League

- **The Disarmament Commission** tried to persuade countries to reduce the size of their armies and the number of their weapons. Persuaded members to ban the use of poison gases in warfare.
- **The Minorities commission** tried to protect minority groups which were being badly treated by the majority in a country (e.g. Muslims in a mainly Christian country.)
- **The Mandates Commission** looked after former German colonies which were taken away from Germany at the end of the war, and governed by Britain, France, Japan, Australia and New Zealand.

Special Committees

- **The Health Organisation** helped countries to work together to prevent the spread of disease. Set new standards for many medicines. Set up research projects into nutrition, child welfare, and public health.
- **The International Labour Organisation** set standards for better working conditions, safety rules and minimum wages. Tried to find ways of reducing unemployment.
- **The Refugee Organisation** helped stateless refugees, e.g. helped half a milion prisoners of war trapped in Russia after the First World War to return home.
- There were also special committees for women's rights, child welfare, and economic and financial affairs.

Peace agreements

As well as joining the League of Nations, a number of countries signed peace pacts, or agreements, with each other. In 1925 France, Belgium and Germany signed the Locarno Pact, promising never to fight each other again. In 1929, sixty-five countries signed the Kellogg Pact, promising never to use war as a way of settling quarrels between them. Sixty countries also agreed to meet in Geneva in 1932 for a disarmament conference. There they would talk about reducing their armed forces and weapons.

Questions

1 Look carefully at Source 1.

  a How many disputes did the League try to settle in the 1920s?
  b How many disputes did it succeed in settling?
  c How many countries were (i) members, and (ii) not members of the League by 1930?
  d How might that have affected the League's ability to keep peace?

2 Look at Source 2. In your own words, describe the different kinds of work that the League of Nations was doing in the 1920s.

3 Judging by the Sources and information on these pages, why do you think so many people in 1929 thought that world peace would last for a long time? Explain your answer.

Why did the Great Depression threaten world peace?

The 1920s were a time of hope that there would never again be a war. In 1929, however, world peace was threatened by the start of a deep economic slump known as the Great Depression. What was the Great Depression, and why did it threaten the peace of the world?

The Great Depression

The Great Depression began in 1929 and lasted until about 1935. During these years, trade between nations dropped. Hundreds of banks closed down. Thousands of companies went out of business. As a result, some 25 million people lost their jobs. Many of the people who lost their jobs also lost their homes, and spent the Depression living in dreadful poverty.

The Depression in Germany

One of the countries hit hardest by the Depression was Germany. At least six million workers in a population of sixty-four million were unemployed by 1933.

Source 1

The spread of dictatorships in the 1930s.

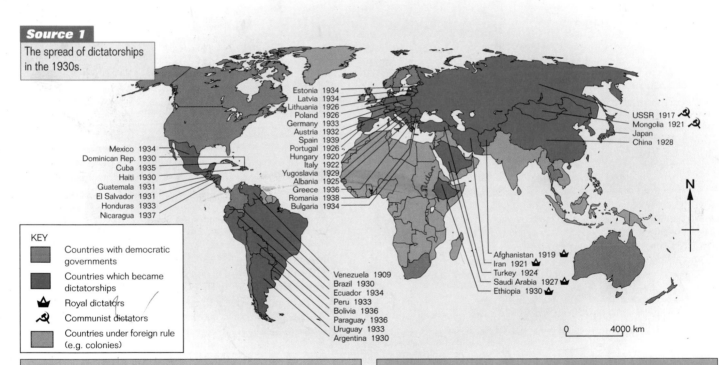

Estonia 1934
Latvia 1934
Lithuania 1926
Poland 1926
Germany 1933
Austria 1932
Spain 1939
Portugal 1926
Hungary 1920
Italy 1922
Yugoslavia 1929
Albania 1925
Greece 1936
Romania 1938
Bulgaria 1934

USSR 1917
Mongolia 1921
Japan
China 1928

Mexico 1934
Dominican Rep. 1930
Cuba 1935
Haiti 1930
Guatemala 1931
El Salvador 1931
Honduras 1933
Nicaragua 1937

Afghanistan 1919
Iran 1921
Turkey 1924
Saudi Arabia 1927
Ethiopia 1930

Venezuela 1909
Brazil 1930
Ecuador 1934
Peru 1933
Bolivia 1936
Paraguay 1936
Uruguay 1933
Argentina 1930

0   4000 km

KEY

- Countries with democratic governments
- Countries which became dictatorships
- Royal dictators
- Communist dictators
- Countries under foreign rule (e.g. colonies)

Democracy

In a democracy, people have a say in how the country is governed:

- They vote in regular elections in which there are several parties to choose from.
- They are represented by the organisations they elect – for example, parliament, or local councils.

They have rights to:

- Freedom of speech (the right to say what they think).
- Freedom of information (the right to read, listen to and watch what they want).
- Freedom of belief (the right to worship freely in their own religion).
- Freedom in law (the right to a fair trial if arrested; freedom from unfair arrest).
- Freedom of association (the right to join or form a political party, trade union or other association).

Dictatorship

In a dictatorship, people have no say in how the country is run:

- There are no regular elections. Usually, only one party is allowed – the one led by the dictator.
- People are represented only by organisations which the dictator allows to exist.

In a dictatorship people have very few rights:

- There is no free speech. If they criticise the dictator or his party they are likely to be arrested.
- There is no freedom of information. The dictator controls the press, books, film etc.
- Not all religions are allowed.
- There is no legal freedom. The police can arrest who they like and keep them in prison without trial.
- People can only join associations allowed by the dictator.

Unemployment and hunger changed the way people thought and behaved. Many blamed the government for their poverty. They started supporting political parties whose leaders promised them work if they were elected to power. One party which made such a promise was the National Socialist Party, or Nazi Party for short. Led by Adolf Hitler, the Nazis won six and a half million votes in an election for the German parliament in 1930.

The more people lost their jobs, the better the Nazis did in elections. In 1932, the worst year of the Depression, the Nazis got 13.5 million votes. This made them the biggest party in the German parliament. The next year, 1933, Adolf Hitler became the head of the German government.

Source 2

Four dictators and their parties.

	Germany	**Italy**	**Soviet Union**	**China**
Dictator:			 (actually id 3 position)	

	Germany	**Italy**	**Soviet Union**	**China**
Dictator:	Adolf Hitler	Benito Mussolini	Joseph Stalin	Chiang Kaishek
Title:	Der Führer (The Leader)	Il Duce (The Leader)	various (e.g. Man of Steel; Universal Genius)	Generalissimo (Supreme Commander)
In power:	1933–45	1922–43	1925–53	1928–49
Party:	Nazi Party (short for National Socialist German Workers' Party)	Fascist Party	Communist Party of the Soviet Union	Guomindang (short for People's National Party)
Symbol of the Party	the swastika	the fasces	the hammer and sickle	
	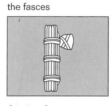			
Armed force of the Party:	Storm Troopers (known as Brownshirts)	Combat Groups (known as Blackshirts)	Red Army	Blueshirts
Main aims and ideas:	• unite all Germans in one country • make Germany bigger • destroy Communism • get rid of racial minority groups (e.g. Jews) • strengthen the German economy	• unite all Italians in one country • make Italy bigger • destroy Communism • strengthen the Italian economy	• strengthen the Soviet economy • strengthen Communism in the USSR • strengthen the Soviet forces	• unite the Chinese in China • make China bigger • destroy Communism • modernise and strengthen the Chinese economy

The spread of dictatorship

Similar things happened in other countries hit by the Depression. Voters blamed their governments for unemployment, and supported parties which promised jobs. As a result, new governments came to power in more than twenty countries during the 1930s.

In many of these countries, the new leaders who took control became dictators. Source 1 explains what a dictator was, and shows the countries which became dictatorships in the 1920s and 1930s. Source 2 compares four of the leading dictators and shows how they ran their countries.

The spread of dictatorship was a threat to world peace because some of these dictators started acting aggressively towards other countries. They did so in an attempt to improve the situation in their own countries. You can find out about their aggression on the next two pages.

Questions

1 Look at Source 1 and read what the words *democracy* and *dictatorship* mean.

  a Which best describes the country you live in? Explain your answer.

  b Look at the map. How many countries became dictatorships after the Great Depression began in 1929?

  c What connection was there between the Depression and the spread of dictatorships?

2 Look at Source 2.

  a What did these dictators have in common?

  b Which aims and ideas of the dictators do you think were a threat to world peace? Explain your answer.

The aggression of the dictators

The countries which acted most aggressively during the Depression were Japan, Italy and Germany (see Source 2). What were their motives, and why did other countries not stop them?

A German cartoon of 1932 shows (1) a Japanese soldier putting up the Japanese flag in Manchuria, (2) the soldier killing a Chinese inhabitant of Manchuria, (3) the League of Nations sending a note to the Japanese army, trying to persuade it to leave Manchuria alone, (4) the Japanese soldier at the end of the war, still in Manchuria.

Japan invades China

Japan was very badly hit by the Depression. By 1931, half her factories were shut. Millions of people were close to starvation. Officers in the Japanese army decided that the quickest way out of the Depression would be to conquer foreign land. This would give Japan raw materials and allow her to increase her trade. This in turn would give people work.

The land they chose to conquer was a province of China called Manchuria. Japanese companies already owned factories, railways and ports there, and a Japanese army was based there to protect them. In 1931, this army took control of the whole of Manchuria.

The League of Nations, whose job was to keep world peace, had three ways of dealing with this kind of aggression. It could try persuasion. It could ask all League members to stop trading with the attacker. Or it could organise a League army to throw the attacker out.

In 1931, no country wanted to stop trading with Japan. The Depression had already damaged world trade. Nobody wanted to damage it further by banning trade with anyone. Nor did any country think it was possible to throw the Japanese out of Manchuria with a League army. The League therefore could only try to persuade them to leave. This did not work. The Japanese simply resigned from the League and went on to occupy even more of China.

Italy invades Ethiopia

Many centuries ago, Italy was the centre of the mighty Roman Empire. The Italian dictator, Mussolini, dreamed of remaking the Empire by conquering foreign lands. His biggest target was Ethiopia, which lay in between two Italian colonies in East Africa.

Italian forces invaded Ethiopia in 1935. The League immediately asked all its members to stop trading with Italy. The aim was to starve Italy's forces of oil, food and weapons. But this ban on trade did not work. The USA, then the world's largest oil producer, was not a member of the League, and so did not stop selling oil to Italy. Italy was able to keep its forces well supplied. By mid-1936 it had conquered the whole country.

Source 2

Acts of aggression in the 1930s.

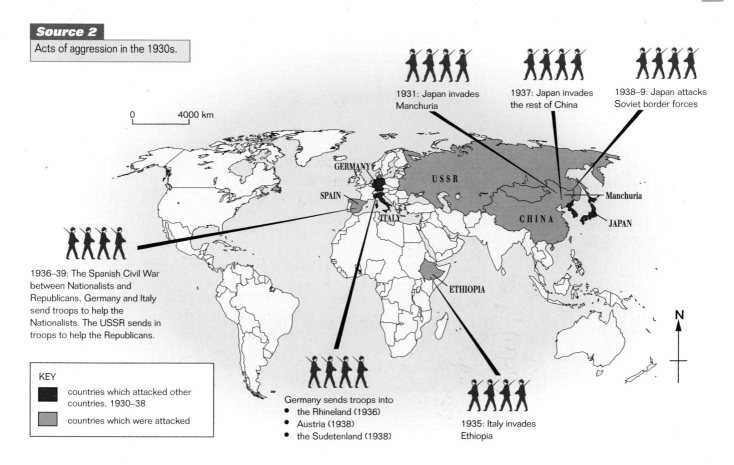

1931: Japan invades Manchuria

1937: Japan invades the rest of China

1938–9: Japan attacks Soviet border forces

1936–39: The Spanish Civil War between Nationalists and Republicans, Germany and Italy send troops to help the Nationalists. The USSR sends in troops to help the Republicans.

KEY

■ countries which attacked other countries, 1930–38

▨ countries which were attacked

Germany sends troops into
• the Rhineland (1936)
• Austria (1938)
• the Sudetenland (1938)

1935: Italy invades Ethiopia

The Spanish Civil War

In 1936 a civil war began in Spain. On one side were the Republicans, who supported the Spanish government. On the other were the Nationalists, who wanted to overthrow it.

The Republicans and the Nationalists had many reasons for fighting. One was a clash of ideas. Republicans believed they were fighting to defend democracy against fascists. Nationalists believed they were defending the Christian Church against communists.

Though there were many reasons for the war, most foreigners thought that this clash of ideas was the most important. They saw the Spanish Civil War as a conflict between democracy and dictatorship. Some 40,000 foreigners went to Spain to fight on the Republican side, believing this would help to save democracy. In several cases, foreign governments also took part in the fighting to help the side whose ideas they supported. Italy and Germany helped the Nationalists. The Soviet Union backed the Republicans.

Most countries, however, decided not to send help. Britain and France feared that if they got involved, the conflict would spread to become a major European war. They set up a Non-intervention Committee in 1936. Most European countries joined it, and agreed not to supply arms to either side.

Backed by Germany and Italy, the Nationalists won the civil war in 1939.

Questions

1 Look at Source 1. Using the information in the text on page 44, write captions for each picture, explaining what real events in Manchuria they portrayed.

2 a What similarity was there between Japan's reason for attacking Manchuria, and Italy's reason for attacking Ethiopia?
b What difference was there between their reasons?

3 For what different reasons did countries not try to stop the aggression of the dictators in Manchuria, Ethiopia and Spain?

The most aggressive of the dictators in the 1930s was the German leader, Adolf Hitler.

Hitler's aims

Hitler had three aims in his dealings with other countries. The first was to get back the land taken from Germany in 1919 (see page 28). The second was to unite all German-speaking people in one country. The third was to make Germany bigger by taking land from other countries.

Occupation of the Rhineland

He began by sending an army into the Rhineland area of Germany. This was forbidden by the Versailles Treaty. It said that the German army must not go nearer than 50 kilometres to the River Rhine. Source 1 helps to explain why Hitler wanted to break the Treaty by occupying the Rhineland.

Hitler risked starting a war by doing this. The Treaty said that Britain and France could use force to stop him. However, the British did not think that German soldiers in the Rhineland were a threat. One government advisor said, 'The Germans are only going into their own back garden.' The French were more worried, but they worked out that a million soldiers would be needed to expel the Germans. They did not want to risk this without Britain's support. Neither, therefore, tried to halt the occupation.

Union with Austria, 1938

Hitler aimed to make Germany and Austria, where most people were German-speakers, into one country. This too was forbidden by the Versailles Treaty, so Hitler had to go about it carefully.

He began by telling Austrian Nazis to make trouble by letting off bombs and starting riots. He wanted it to look as if the government could not control the country. As Hitler intended, the police could not halt the violence, so he said he would send the German army to Austria to 'restore order'. The Austrian leader could not find a way of protecting his country from this threat, so he resigned. An Austrian Nazi took his place, and asked Hitler to send in the German army. German soldiers thus marched into Austria by invitation. Soon after, Hitler made Germany and Austria into one country.

Source 1

This German postcard was produced in 1935. Find the River Rhine, and the area either side of it, known as the Rhineland (shown in yellow). The aim of the postcard was to persuade British people that Germany's armed forces had been reduced unfairly by the Treaty of Versailles.

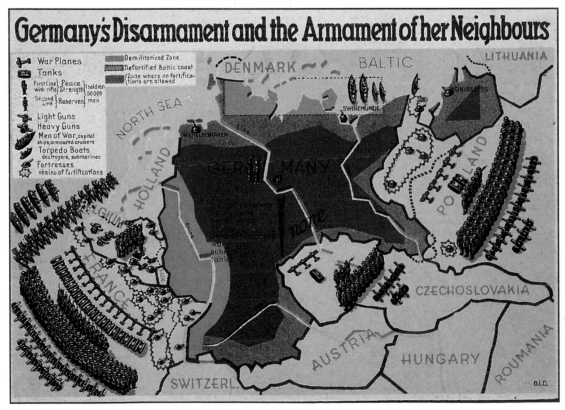

Germany's Disarmament and the Armament of her Neighbours

Appeasement at Munich

However, the leaders of France and Britain did not want war. Britain's Prime Minister, Neville Chamberlain, flew to Germany to discuss the matter. Hitler told him that the Sudetenland was the last piece of land he wanted.

Chamberlain and Hitler, along with the leaders of France and Italy, then met in Munich to settle the matter. They agreed that the Czechs should give the Sudetenland to Germany. The Czechs had to agree to this. If they did not agree, they would have to fight Germany alone. On 1 October 1938 German forces marched into the Sudetenland.

Chamberlain's negotiations with Hitler in 1938 were known as appeasement. This meant giving in to some of Hitler's demands in order to avoid going to war. Source 3 shows one of the main reasons why Chamberlain appeased Hitler instead of using force against him.

Occupation of the Sudetenland, 1938

Hitler used the same trick to take an area of Czechoslovakia called the Sudetenland, where three million German-speaking people lived. He ordered his supporters there to stage riots and demonstrations, so that it would look as if the Czechs could not control their own country. He then sent the German army to the border, and ordered the Czechs to give up the area.

The Czechs refused, and prepared to defend themselves. They not only had a strong army but could also count on the support of two allies, France and the USSR. It looked as if a German attack on Czechoslovakia would lead to a war involving at least four countries.

Source 2

This Swiss cartoon, drawn in 1938, shows Hitler as the giant, Gulliver, surrounded by Lilliputians with the names of Europe's leading politicians. On the sole of Hitler's boot is the Nazi slogan *'Sieg Heil'* (Hail Victory). Find Neville Chamberlain (bottom right), French politicians (bottom left), and members of the League of Nations looking at the Treaty of Versailles (left).

Source 3

From a speech by Neville Chamberlain in 1938, two months before he went to Germany for talks with Hitler.

When I think of those four terrible years (1914-18) and I think of the seven million young men who were cut down in their prime, the thirteen million who were maimed and mutilated, the misery and suffering of the mothers and fathers, the sons and daughters of those who were killed, and the wounded, then I am bound to say...in war...there are no winners, but all are losers. It is those thoughts which have made me...strain every nerve to avoid a repetition of the Great War in Europe.

Questions

1. Look at Source 1.

   a. How does the postcard try to persuade British people that the German armed forces had been reduced unfairly by the Treaty of Versailles?

   b. How does the postcard explain why Hitler wanted an army in the Rhineland?

2. Look at Source 2.

   a. What did Hitler do in 1938 that made him appear like a giant in Europe?

   b. Why did the British and French politicians, shown as little people, not use force to stop Hitler?

   c. What does the cartoonist's opinion of the politicians seem to have been?

3. Read Source 3. In your own words, explain why Neville Chamberlain appeased Hitler instead of stopping him from taking the Sudetenland.

1939: sliding into war again

When he returned from Munich in 1938, Neville Chamberlain announced 'It is peace for our time' (see Source 1). Only eleven months later, Britain went to war with Germany, and a Second World War began. What happened during those months to bring about war so soon after Chamberlain promised peace?

Hitler invades Czechoslovakia

At the Munich Conference, Hitler said that the Sudetenland was the last piece of land he wanted. But Hitler lied to Chamberlain. Six months later, in March 1939, his army marched into the rest of Czechoslovakia. Half the country (called Bohemia-Moravia) was made into part of Germany. The other half became a new state called Slovakia.

Chamberlain now realised that Hitler could not be trusted. He decided that Hitler must be stopped from taking any more land. It was easy to see where Hitler would strike next. He wanted an area of Poland known as the Polish Corridor which had been taken from Germany in 1919 (see page 31). It was the only piece of land taken in 1919 that Hitler had not yet taken back. Chamberlain promised that Britain would help defend Poland against Germany. The government of France joined in this promise.

Europe splits into two enemy camps

Despite the new, tough stand of Britain and France, Hitler carried on building up his armed forces. Then he made an agreement with the dictator of Italy, Mussolini, that they would help each other in any war. By early summer 1939, therefore, Europe was divided into two enemy camps. Britain and France were in one camp, saying they would protect Poland. Germany and Italy were in the other, and Germany looked sure to attack Poland.

This worried the leader of the Soviet Union, Stalin. He knew that Hitler hated the Soviet Union because it was a communist country. He knew also that Hitler wanted extra land in eastern Europe. He feared that a German attack on Poland would be followed by a German attack on the Soviet Union.

Stalin therefore looked for help. He offered to join Britain and France in their alliance to protect Poland. But the British and French did not trust him. Talks between them quickly broke down.

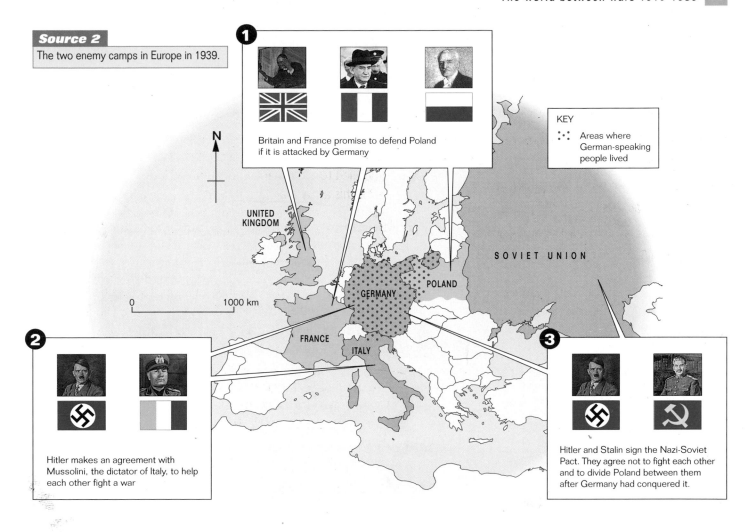

Source 2

The two enemy camps in Europe in 1939.

Britain and France promise to defend Poland if it is attacked by Germany

KEY

Areas where German-speaking people lived

N

0   1000 km

UNITED KINGDOM

SOVIET UNION

GERMANY   POLAND

FRANCE

ITALY

Hitler makes an agreement with Mussolini, the dictator of Italy, to help each other fight a war

Hitler and Stalin sign the Nazi-Soviet Pact. They agree not to fight each other and to divide Poland between them after Germany had conquered it.

The Nazi-Soviet Pact

Stalin instead turned for help to the man he trusted least: Hitler. They signed an agreement not to fight each other if there was a war in Poland. In secret, they also promised to divide Poland between them after it was conquered.

This Nazi-Soviet Pact amazed everyone. Overnight, two enemies had agreed not to fight each other. But their reasons for doing it soon became clear. Stalin signed it so that he could be safe from Germany while he built up his forces. Hitler signed it so that he could attack Poland without having to worry that the Soviet army would try to stop him. Only a week after the two dictators had signed the Pact, the German army invaded Poland. Soviet forces invaded soon after. Between them they took over the entire country.

Declarations of war

Britain and France now honoured their promise to Poland. On 3 September 1939 they declared war on Germany and its ally, Italy. And because Britain and France had great empires in Africa, Asia and the Far East, the war would soon spread from Europe to these other parts of the world, making it a world war.

Questions

1 Look at Source 2.

   a What information on the map shows why Poland was likely to be Hitler's next victim in 1939?

   b If Britain and France had allowed the Soviet Union to join them in the agreement to defend Poland, how would this have affected Hitler's plans for invading Poland?

   c Why did Hitler's pact with the Soviet Union make it much easier for Hitler to attack Poland?

2 Neville Chamberlain said 'It is peace in our time' in September 1938.

   a Why did he think this?

   b What was the main reason why his prediction turned out to be wrong?

   c What do you think would have most helped to ensure a lasting peace in 1939?

Depth Study

5 Nazi Germany

Imagine that you are German. You are walking along the street sixty years ago. You recognise a group of people walking towards you. This is what a German newspaper of 1935 says you should do:

> If people belong to the same social group, raise the right arm at an angle so that the palm of the hand can be seen. The appropriate phrase that goes with it is 'Heil Hitler' or at least 'Heil'. If one meets a person…inferior to oneself, then the right arm is to be fully stretched out; raised to eye-level. At the same time, one is to say 'Heil Hitler'.

During the twelve years that Adolf Hitler ruled Germany, from 1933 to 1945, millions of Germans greeted each other every day in this way. The scene in the picture below could have been photographed almost anywhere at any time in Germany.

How was one man able to get such control over 60 million Germans that they saluted and said his name whenever they met? This part of the book tries to answer that question by looking closely at Germany during the 1930s. Let us begin by finding out what kind of person Hitler was, and the kind of people who supported him.

Source 1

Office workers and customers in a bank in Munich give the 'Hitler salute' as they listen to a speech on a public radio.

Who were the Nazis?

Adolf Hitler was born in Austria. In Source 2, he describes his early life in his own words.

Hitler was 25 when the First World War began. He joined the German army at the very start of the war, and spent the whole of the war on active service. Source 3 gives us an idea of what kind of soldier he was.

Hitler was very angry when Germany surrendered in 1918. He called the politicians who surrendered 'November Criminals'. Soon after, he joined a small political party, and quickly became its leader. He named it the National Socialist German Workers' Party, or Nazi Party for short.

The Nazi Party grew rapidly. It started with 50 members in 1919 and grew to 3000 in 1920, 6000 in 1921 and nearly 60,000 in 1923. Source 4 shows the kind of people who joined between 1920 and 1923.

Source 2

This is part of a letter which Hitler wrote in 1921. He was replying to an admirer who wrote to him, asking for information about his background.

I was born on 20 April, 1889, in Braunau am Inn, the son of a local post official, Alois Hitler. My entire schooling consisted of five years of Primary School and four years of Middle School.... I was orphaned at the age of seventeen and...was forced to earn my living as a simple worker. I became a labourer on a building site and during the next two years did every imaginable type of casual labour....

With tremendous effort I was able to teach myself to paint, and ... from the age of 20 I earned a living by this work.... In 1912 I moved to Munich where I worked at this profession. During the first four years of my stay, from the age of 20 to 24, I became more and more involved in politics.

Source 3

A report on Hitler by the commanding officer of the army regiment in which he served.

Lance-Corporal (Volunteer) Hitler, Third Company.

Hitler has been with the regiment since the beginning of the war. He has given a splendid account of himself in all the battles in which he has taken part.

As company-runner* he ... was always ready to volunteer to carry messages in the most difficult positions and at great risk to his life.

Hitler received the Iron Cross** (second class) for gallant conduct in the Battle of Wytschaete on 2 December 1914. I regard him as fully worthy to be decorated with the Iron Cross (first class).

*company runner: a messenger
**Iron Cross: the highest medal awarded by the German army

Source 4

The social class and occupations of people who joined the Nazi Party, 1920-23.

Class	Occupation	% of total
Working class	Unskilled workers (e.g. labourers, miners)	11.9
	Skilled workers (e.g. bakers, plumbers)	24.0
Middle class	Master craftsmen (e.g. watchmakers, tailors)	8.3
	Lower employees (e.g. shop assistants, clerks)	11.8
	Lower civil servants (e.g. post office workers)	6.6
	Merchants (e.g. car dealers, wholesalers)	14.4
	Farmers (e.g. farm-owners, wine-makers)	11.0
Upper middle class and aristocracy	Managers (e.g. company executives)	1.9
	Higher civil servants (e.g. tax officers)	0.4
	Professionals (e.g. doctors, lawyers, architects)	2.5
	Entrepreneurs (e.g. company directors, factory owners)	2.7
	Students (senior school pupils and university students)	4.4

What attracted these people to the Nazi Party? One reason for its success was Hitler's ability to put his ideas across to the public at mass meetings. Sources 5, 6 and 7 show how he did this. The Nazis also put across their ideas through newspapers (see Sources 8 and 9). An eye-catching symbol, the swastika, also helped to gain publicity (see Source 9).

As the Nazi Party grew, it also created enemies. Communists especially opposed the Nazis, and often tried to break up their meetings. The Nazis created an armed, uniformed force of 'Storm Troopers', the *Sturm Abteilung*, or SA, to fight their opponents and protect their meetings (see Source 10).

Source 5

Stills from a film that Hitler made of himself in 1922, practising a speech.

Source 6

Carl Zuckmayer, a Communist, describes a Nazi Party meeting that he went to in 1923. The extract is taken from his memoirs, published in 1970.

He knew how to whip up those crowds jammed closely in a dense cloud of cigarette smoke and sausage smells - not by arguments but by his fanatical manner.... He would draw up a list of existing evils and imaginary wrongs, and after listing them in a louder and louder voice, he screamed 'And whose fault is it?' He would follow it up with the reply: 'It's all / the fault / of the Jews.'

The beer mugs would swiftly take up the beat, crashing down on the wooden tables, and thousands of voices repeated the idiotic line for a quarter of an hour.

Source 7

Kurt Ludecke, a former Nazi, describes a Nazi mass meeting in 1922. The extract is taken from his memoirs, published in 1938.

Red placards announced in huge black letters that he (Hitler) was to appear.... Here were inflammatory slogans. 'Versailles: Germany's ruin...Republic of the People or State of the Jews?... Down with the November Criminals....' And every one of his placards ended with the phrase 'Jews not admitted'....

When the man stepped forward on the platform...he stood silent for a moment. Then he began to speak, quietly at first. Before long his voice had risen to a hoarse shriek....

He urged the revival of German honour and manhood in a blast of words .... Then he accused the leaders in Berlin of being 'November Criminals'. 'Germany must be free!' was his final, defiant slogan. Then two last words rang out like the sting of a lash: 'Awake Germany!' There was thunderous applause.

Source 8

The aims of the Nazi Party, summarised in the German newspaper *Kreuzzeitung*, 28 December 1922.

> Hitler is in close contact with the Germans of Czechoslovakia and Austria, and he demands the union of all Germans in greater Germany....
>
> With the same energy, Hitler demands the cancellation of the Treaty of Versailles....
>
> He wants only people of German race to be citizens of Germany. Those who are not would not be allowed into public employment.... He wants all immigrants to Germany since 1914 to be expelled.
>
> Hitler opposes the parliamentary system.... Hitler's party wants above all to set up a dictatorship.... The dictator would be Hitler.

Source 9

from the *Völkischer Beobachter* (the Nazi Party newspaper), 22 March 1923.

> The red stands for the kind of people who belong to our party (workers), the white is the symbol of our love for the German fatherland. The black swastika stands for our struggle against any damned foreign race which tries to pull our country down.

Source 10

A Nazi recruiting poster for the SA (*Sturm Abteilung)*, or Storm Troopers.

Reichswettkampf der SA

Questions

1. Look at Source 4.
   a. What four groups of people were most likely to join the Nazis in 1923?
   b. What kind of people were least likely to join the Nazi Party?

2. Read Sources 6, 7, 8 and 9. What were the main ideas of Hitler and the Nazis?

3. a. Use Sources 2 and 5 to describe the sort of person you think Hitler was.
   b. How can you tell from Source 6 that Carl Zuckmayer did not support Hitler?

4. What kind of person do you think might have joined the SA (Source 10)?

How did Hitler become leader of Germany?

In 1923 Hitler tried to overthrow the government by starting a revolution. He failed. Police shot sixteen Nazis dead. Hitler was arrested and sent to prison. But this did not kill the party. From his prison cell, Hitler plotted the government's overthrow. Less than ten years later he was leader of Germany. How was able to achieve this?

The Nazis in the 'golden twenties'

Hitler was released from prison after only a year for good behaviour. For the next four years he recruited new members for the party. He set up new party branches all over the country. He campaigned in elections. This had little effect, however. Between 1924 and 1929 the German economy was growing. Many people's living standards were improving. Germans called these years 'the golden twenties'.

The Nazis in the Depression

In 1929, however, the Great Depression began (see page 42). The 'golden twenties' gave way to mass unemployment and hunger. Many Germans blamed the government for this. They gave their support to parties which said they could end the Depression. Source 1 is an example of this. As a result, support for the Nazi Party soared (see Source 2).

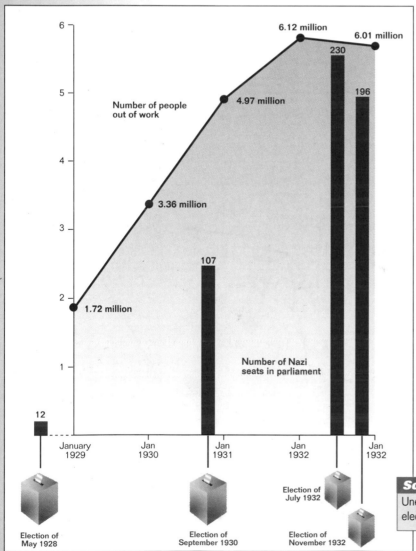

Source 1

Written by a worker in 1934 in a prize essay contest for 'the best personal life history of a Nazi'. The contest was organised by an American researcher who was trying to find out why people became Nazis.

...The breakdown (*i.e. the Depression*) threatened to bring all economic life to a standstill. Thousands of factories closed their doors. Hunger was the daily companion of the German working man.... Many an honest working man had to resort to theft to obtain food.... All fellow citizens...yearned for better times. As for me, like many another, I had lost all I possessed...so, early in 1930, I joined the National Socialist Party.

Source 2

Unemployment and the Nazi vote in elections for parliament, 1929-1932.

The Nazis used many different methods to put their ideas across to the public. One method was propaganda. This is a form of advertising which tries to change the way people think. Source 3 shows the most common form of propaganda which they used - the political poster. Nazi ideas were also spread by millions of pamphlets and by eight Nazi-owned newspapers.

As nobody had a television at that time, politicians held mass meetings to put ideas across to audiences. Source 4 shows Hitler speaking at a mass meeting in 1932, asking people to vote Nazi. His private army, the SA, stood guard at such meetings. They often also smashed up the meetings of rival parties, especially the Communists.

The 1932 elections

In an election in July 1932 the Nazis became Germany's largest party. They won 230 of the 608 seats in parliament. This put Hitler in a strong position. The government would need the support of those 230 Nazis whenever it asked parliament to vote for new laws.

The Chancellor, who was leader of the government, offered Hitler posts in the government in return for his support. Hitler refused. He said he wanted the Chancellor's job. The Chancellor therefore held another election, trying to get more seats for his own party. Although the Nazis won fewer seats (196) in this second election, they were still the largest party.

The German President, Hindenburg, did not want Hitler to be Chancellor. He feared that Hitler would become a dictator. However, the elections had put so many Nazis into parliament that the government could not work without their support. Hindenburg had no choice. Reluctantly, he made Hitler Chancellor on 30 January 1933.

Source 3

A Nazi election poster of 1932. It says 'Women! Millions of men are out of work. Millions of children have no future. Save our German families. Vote for Adolf Hitler!'

Source 4

Hitler speaking at a mass meeting in Munich during the 1932 election campaign. Notice the SA men, wearing peaked caps, facing the audience. The banner says 'Support Adolf Hitler. Vote National Socialist (i.e. Nazi)'.

Questions

1 Look at Source 2. Describe in words what the graph shows.

2 Use the information and Sources on these pages to explain the increase in the Nazi vote shown in Source 2.

How did Hitler become a dictator?

When Hitler became Chancellor in 1933, he was leader of a democratic country, sharing power with an elected President and parliament. Eighteen months later he was a dictator, sharing power with nobody. How did Hitler do this?

The election of 1933

When he became Chancellor, Hitler's powers were limited. Only three government ministers were Nazis, and the Nazi Party had less than half the seats in parliament. Hitler therefore arranged another election, hoping to get more than half the seats in parliament. Using all kinds of propaganda, as well as mass meetings and parades, the Nazis aimed for a big win.

The Nazi election campaign was given a boost by an unexpected event. The parliament building burnt down (see Source 1). A communist was caught at the scene of the blaze. Hitler claimed that this was a communist plot against the government. He asked President Hindenburg to give him extra power to deal with the threat. Believing that Germany was in danger, Hindenburg allowed the Nazis to take action against the Communists. They arrested 4000 Communists, shut down communist newspapers and broke up communist meetings. This ruined the Communists' election campaign.

The election was held on 5 March. It gave the Nazis more seats than before, but they still had less than half. Hitler overcame this problem by joining forces with another, smaller party, the Nationalists. Their 58 seats, added to the Nazis' 288, amounted to just over half the seats in parliament. Hitler could now be sure that parliament would vote for the laws he wanted.

Source 1

The German parliament in Berlin on fire, 27 February 1933.

DEUTSCHEN VOLKE

The Enabling Law

Hitler put the first of his laws to the vote on 23 March. It was called the 'Enabling Law'. It gave Hitler the power until 1937 to make laws without asking parliament for approval. To put it another way, the Enabling Law gave Hitler the power of a dictator for the next four years.

Now that Hitler could make his own laws, he reorganised the way Germany was governed. Germany was made up of eighteen states, each with its own local parliament, police and laws. In April, Hitler appointed new State Governors to each state. All eighteen were Nazis. Later, in January 1934, Hitler got rid of the state parliaments.

Hitler then turned on the trade unions. On 2 May 1933, Nazis broke into trade union offices all over Germany and arrested thousands of officials. The unions were then merged into a 'German Labour Front', led by a Nazi.

Next, rival political parties were banned. On 10 May, Nazis took over the offices of the Social Democratic Party, the country's second largest party, and confiscated its funds. Two weeks later they confiscated the property of the Communist Party. In June, the same thing happened to all the smaller parties. By July, only one party remained in existence, the Nazi Party.

The Night of the Long Knives

By 1934 the only rivals of Hitler still left were in the Nazi Party itself, and in the SA. The SA, as you have read, was the private army of the Nazi Party. Ernst Röhm, leader of the SA, wanted to merge the SA with the German army, with both under his control. This alarmed Hitler. A merger of the two would make Röhm the most powerful man in Germany.

On Hitler's orders, Röhm and the other SA chiefs were arrested during the night of 30 June 1934. They were taken to prison and shot dead. Nazis described these killings as 'the Night of the Long Knives'.

Hitler becomes Führer

Only weeks after the Night of the Long Knives, President Hindenburg died. Instead of holding elections for a new President, Hitler combined the offices of Chancellor and President into a single post, which he gave to himself. His new title was 'Führer and Reich Chancellor'.

On the same day, 2 August 1934, Hitler made every soldier in the German army swear an oath of personal loyalty to him. They said 'I will give total obedience to Adolf Hitler, the Führer of the German people'. In taking this oath, the only people with any power to oppose Hitler - soldiers with guns - had sworn their lives to his service.

Questions

1 Ask your teacher for Copymaster 22.

   a Study the text on these two pages and find ten events which increased Hitler's power between January 1933 and August 1934.

   b Write down each event on the copymaster next to the date when it happened.

   c Which event do you consider (i) the most important, (ii) the least important in helping Hitler to get more power?

2 Sources 1 and 2 both show fires.

   a Explain how each fire helped Hitler and the Nazis to get more power.

   b Which fire do you think was more important in helping Hitler to get more power? Explain your answer.

What was life like in Nazi Germany?

Hitler had three main aims. One was to get Germany out of the Depression. Another was make Germany powerful again. The third was to create a 'pure German' society by getting rid of minorities such as Jews. Following these three aims changed the lives of millions of people. What was life like for them?

Work and bread

At least seven million Germans were out of work when Hitler came to power. He had promised these people 'work and bread' in the election campaigns. Now he had to find them jobs.

He began by setting up a National Labour Service. This gave young men jobs that needed manual labour, such as digging ditches on farms. All men aged 18 to 25 had to spend six months in the Service. As a result, the unemployment figures dropped rapidly. Source 1 gives an idea of what life in the Labour Service was like for these men.

Another of Hitler's aims was to build up the armed forces. This had a big impact on unemployment. From 1935 onwards, all 18 to 25 year-olds had to do military service for two years. In just five years the army grew from 100,000 to 1,400,000. This cut over a million from the jobless figures (see Source 2).

Source 1

A road worker in the National Labour Service, talking about his work in 1935.

> We work outside in all kinds of weather, shovelling dirt for 51 pfennigs (pence) an hour. Then there are deductions and ... and 15 pfennigs a day for a straw mattress in a draughty wooden barracks, and 35 pfennigs for what they call dinner - slop you wouldn't touch...

Source 3

John Heartfield, a German artist, made this picture in 1935 by cutting up and rearranging photographs. The people are saying 'Hurrah, the butter is all gone!' as they eat bullets, parts of guns and other metal objects.

Source 2

Unemployment, 1929-1939.

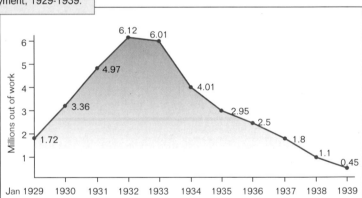

Guns or butter?

Building up the armed forces was very expensive. To help pay for it, Hitler tried to make Germany self-sufficient. This meant replacing things bought from other countries with artificial substitutes. For example, cloth was made from pulped wood grown in Germany instead of from Indian cotton. Coffee was made from acorns, petrol from coal, and make-up from flour.

There were no substitutes for some things, so Germans ran short of some basic goods and foods. Animal fats such as butter and milk were in very short supply. But, as a leading Nazi, Hermann Goering, said in a speech in 1936 'Would you rather have butter or guns? I tell you, guns make us powerful. Butter only makes us fat.' Source 3 shows how a leading German artist made fun of this speech.

This table compares how much food and drink the average working class family consumed in 1927, before Hitler came to power, with consumption four years after he came to power.

	1927	1937		1927	1937
Rye bread (kg)	262.9	316.1	Fish (kg)	21.8	20.4
White bread (kg)	55.2	30.8	Vegetables (kg)	117.2	109.6
Beef and veal (kg)	21.6	21.4	Potatoes (kg)	499.5	519.8
Other meats (kg)	133.7	109.2	Sugar (kg)	47.2	45.0
Bacon (kg)	9.5	8.5	Tropical fruit (kg)	9.7	6.1
Butter (kg)	15.7	18.0	Coffee (kg)	3.3	3.8
Milk (litres)	427.8	367.2	Beer (litres)	76.5	31.6
Eggs (number)	404.0	237.0	Cigarettes (number)	450.0	503.0

Racism

Hitler and the Nazis believed that the German people were a '*volk*', or race, distinct from and superior to other races. They wanted to preserve what they called the 'purity' of the German race. This meant restricting other races in Germany, especially Jews.

The Nazis started to attack Jews as soon as they came to power. They stopped people from using Jewish shops (see Source 5). They sacked thousands of Jews from government jobs. In 1935 two new laws, the Nuremburg Laws, barred Jews from being German citizens and took away some of their most basic rights (see Source 6). Further laws over the next five years stripped Jews of every other right and freedom.

Nazi 'stormtroopers' stand outside a Jewish grocer's shop on 1 April 1933, stopping shoppers from entering. Their placard says 'Germans, do not buy from Jews'.

The 'Nuremburg Laws' of 1935.

The Reich Law on citizenship, 15 September 1935.

A citizen of the Reich is a subject who only has German blood.

Law for the protection of German blood and honour, 15 September 1935

1 Marriages between Jews and citizens of German...blood are forbidden...
2 Sexual relations outside marriage between Jews and nationals of German or kindred blood are forbidden...

Questions

1 'Unemployed people benefitted from Nazi rule.'
   a How does Source 1 go against this view?
   b How does Source 2 support this view?

2 a Why did Hermann Goering say that Germans needed guns more than butter?
   b Look at Source 3. How does the artist make fun of what Goering said?
   c Does Source 4 show that Germans had to eat less because of Nazi policy?

3 a You are a citizen of your country. What rights does this give you?
   b Look at Source 6. What would you lose if your citizenship was taken away by a laws like these?

To achieve his aims quickly, Hitler needed complete obedience from the German people. Everybody therefore found they were being controlled more and more by the Nazi Party, the police and government.

Source 7

This poster of 1937 shows what Nazis thought a woman's role was - to have babies (centre), to look after men and to go to church (background).

Party control

The job of controlling people was shared by the police and the Nazi Party. Around 400,000 local party officials kept watch on every street and every block of flats in every town and city. They snooped on their neighbours and reported suspicious behaviour to their bosses. Criminals and political opponents could be easily identified and turned over to the police.

The Nazis also controlled people through Party organisations. Boys and girls, for example, had to belong to Nazi youth organisations such as the Hitler Youth. There, young people were taught to accept Nazi ideas without question. Source 8 is an example of what they were taught.

Source 8

Extract from the rule book of the Hitler Youth Movement. It describes what a 10- to 14-year-old boy had to do to get a 'badge of achievement'.

The following are conditions for bestowal of the badge:

(1) Indoctrination

   1 Life of the Führer   4 Holidays of the German people
   2 Germans abroad   5 Five flag oaths
   3 Lost territories   6 Six Hitler Youth songs

(2) Athletic achievements

   1 Running, 60m   10 seconds   4 Pull up on the bar twice
   2 Long jump   3.25 metres   5 Somersault twice backwards
   3 Ball throwing   35 metres   6 Swimming 100 metres

(3) Hiking and camping

   1 A day's hike of 15 km with a light pack (not over 5kg).
   2 Participation in a camp living in tents for at least three days.
   3 Put up a pup tent and help put up a barge tent.
   4 Construct a cooking pit; fetch water for cooking.
   5 Know the names of the most important trees.
   6 Ability to orient a map from the stars.

(4) Target practice

   Shooting with an air gun, distance 8m in sitting position: a bull's eye.

Women

In Nazi eyes, a woman's most important job was to bear children, especially boys. Germany's birth rate was falling. The Nazis wanted to reverse that to provide the army with soldiers.

Women were therefore encouraged to have children. The government raised maternity benefits and introduced family allowances. It gave loans to newly married couples which they could keep if they had more than four children. Propaganda such as Source 7 portrayed the ideal woman as someone who looked after the 'three Ks' - *kinder, kirche, kuche* (children, church, cooking).

Controlling public opinion

Whether or not people belonged to the Party, the Nazis tried to control their thinking. The government controlled the media - newspapers, films, radio, plays, cinema and books - and made sure they put across Nazi ideas. Source 9 shows how Nazi control could reach even into people's homes.

The Nazis even restricted the activities of the churches. Catholic schools and monasteries were shut down. Many Catholic priests were arrested. Protestant churches were united to form a 'Reich Church' led by a Nazi bishop. People were even encouraged to become pagans, worshipping the sun instead of the Christian God. Source 10 gives an idea of the beliefs of the largest pagan sect, the German Faith Movement.

Source 9

The Führer speaks. A German artist, Paul Mathias Padua, painted this scene in 1937. It shows a family listening to a radio speech by Hitler. Notice the portrait of Hitler on the wall.

Source 10

Part of a sermon preached on Christmas Eve 1936 in a church of the 'German Faith Movement'.

Christmas is the feast of light of our ancestors.... Between 23rd and 25th of the Yule month *(December)*...each family met under a tree in the woods. The Winter Man, Old Ruprecht...appeared and gave out gifts. Burning torches were attached to a tree and soon the darkness was lit up.... Having sung some Christmas songs, our forefathers went home with the knowledge and joy in their hearts that...they were not forgotten or foresaken by their God. From now on the sun rose higher and higher every day.

Just as our ancestors did not lose their faith in the coming light...so we stand today in the light after long darkness. Germany, after the Great War, was threatened with collapse. But then...happened that greatest miracle: Germany awoke and followed that sign of light, the swastika.

Questions

1 Study Source 8. What do you think the Nazis were trying to achieve by encouraging 10 to 14 year-old boys to do these things?

2 a Compare the pagan Christmas story in Source 10 with the Christian story of Christmas. What similarities and differences are there between them?

   b Suggest what the preacher was trying to achieve with this sermon.

3 A leading Nazi said in 1937, 'The only people who have a private life in Germany today are those who are asleep'. Use the information and Sources on pages 56-61 to give examples of how people's private lives were affected by Nazi rule.

6 The Second World War

How was Germany able to conquer Europe so quickly ?

The Second World War began in 1939 when German forces attacked Poland. In 1940 they went on to conquer six other countries. (See source 2). How were they able to conquer so much of Europe so quickly

Blitzkrieg in Poland

The German forces invaded Poland on 1 September 1939. Using a new method of warfare called *blitzkrieg*, they took only a week to smash the Polish army. Source 1 shows how *blitzkrieg* worked. By November German and Soviet forces had occupied the whole country. Later, the Soviets also took the Baltic States (Estonia, Latvia, Lithuania) and Finland.

Although Britain and France had promised to protect Poland, they were too far away to stop the invasion. So, for the next eight months, they did no fighting. Instead they waited and prepared for war. People called this the 'phoney war'.

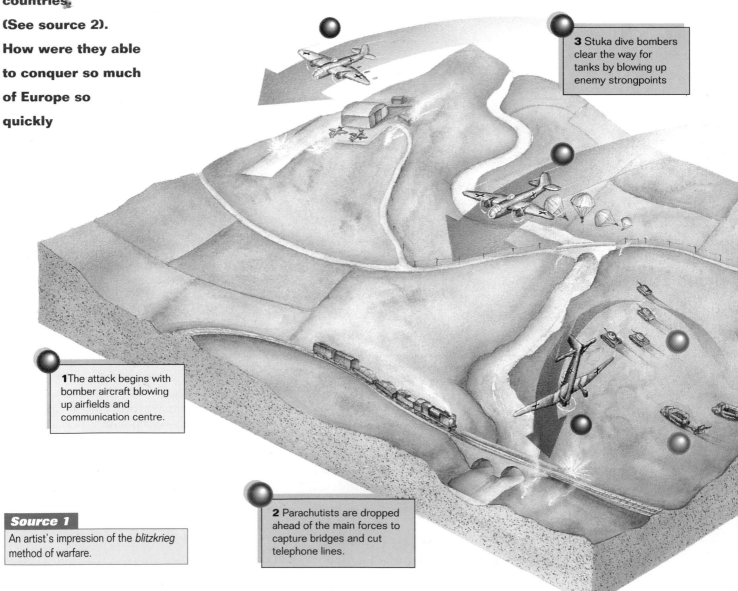

3 Stuka dive bombers clear the way for tanks by blowing up enemy strongpoints

1 The attack begins with bomber aircraft blowing up airfields and communication centre.

2 Parachutists are dropped ahead of the main forces to capture bridges and cut telephone lines.

Source 1

An artist's impression of the *blitzkrieg* method of warfare.

Germany invades Norway and Denmark

In April 1940 the Germans invaded Norway. They did so because the British laid mines along Norway's coast to stop iron ore being taken from Sweden to Germany (see Source 2). As the Germans needed iron for making weapons, they could not afford to have this route blocked. At the same time as taking Norway, the Germans also took Denmark. They needed supply bases there for the invasion of Norway.

Britain sent 30,000 troops to stop the invasion. But they were poorly trained and poorly equipped. Within weeks, they were forced to retreat.

Source 2

The German and Soviet conquest of Europe, 1939-40.

KEY

land occupied by Germany

land occupied by USSR

German invasions

Soviet invasions

Italian attack on France

Route of ships taking iron ore to Germany

SWEDEN
FINLAND — Nov 1939
NORWAY
April 1940
DENMARK
HOLLAND
EIRE
BELGIUM
UNITED KINGDOM
ESTONIA — June 1940
LATVIA
LITHUANIA
SOVIET UNION
17 Sept. 1939
Channel Islands — Dunkirk
May 1940
1 Sept. 1939
POLAND
June 1940
Ardennes Forest
Maginot Line
GREATER GERMANY
SLOVAKIA
HUNGARY
SWITZ.
FRANCE
ITALY
YUGOSLAVIA
ROMANIA
SPAIN
BULGARIA

4 Tanks, travelling at 30 to 40 km per hour, smash through weak spots in the enemy's defences. They are followed by infantry travelling in armoured troop carriers.

Germany attacks the West

A month later, Hitler's forces attacked western Europe. His aim was to smash France and force Britain to surrender. Using *blitzkrieg*, they invaded Belgium and Holland on 10 May. They defeated them in just three weeks.

This left France open to attack. Since the First World War, France had built a chain of massive fortresses along its border with Germany. They were known as the Maginot Line (see Source 2). But now that the Germans had taken Belgium, they were able to attack through the Ardennes forest, avoiding the Maginot Line. The French forces there were weak and poorly trained. They could not stop the Germans from breaking through into France.

The Germans now swept through north-east France at high speed. They forced the British and French armies facing them to retreat to Dunkirk. Italian forces attacked southern France at the same time. The French surrendered, and German forces occupied northern France as well as the Channel Islands.

Questions

1 Find Source 6 on page 12 and Source 2 on page 25. Compare them with Source 1 on this page.

a Look at Source 1. Explain in your own words how the *blitzkrieg* method of warfare worked.

b Find Source 6. Between 1914 and 1918 the Germans did not conquer much land. Just over twenty years later, they conquered six European countries in only nine months. Using these Sources, explain why the Germans were able to do this in 1939-40 but not in 1914-18.

2 For what different reasons were the British and French unable to stop the invasion of Poland, Norway and France?

Why was Britain not defeated in 1940?

After beating and occupying France in June 1940, the Germans prepared to invade Britain. The British army in France had just been defeated, and Britain was very weak. Yet the German invasion failed. Why was Britain not defeated in 1940?

Source 1

From a speech by Winston Churchill in the House of Commons, on 13 May 1940.

I have nothing to offer but blood, toil, tears and sweat.... You ask, what is our policy? I will say: it is to wage war, by sea, land and air, with all our might.... You ask, what is our aim? I can answer in one word. Victory ... however long and hard the road may be.

Source 2

This picture was painted by a British artist. It shows British and French soldiers being rescued from the beaches at Dunkirk in 1940.

A new leader: Winston Churchill

Some British people thought that Britain would have to make peace, leaving Germany in control of Europe. But Britain now had a new Prime Minister, Winston Churchill. He replaced Neville Chamberlain, who resigned in May 1940. Churchill refused to surrender. Source 1 gives an idea of his attitude.

Evacuation from Dunkirk

When the Germans invaded France, the British and French forces there retreated to the Channel coast. Nearly half a million British and French soldiers were trapped between the sea and the advancing Germans.

At the last moment, the British navy organised a massive rescue operation. Several hundred warships sailed to the French coast in 'Operation Dynamo'. They were helped by volunteers in hundreds of small boats such as trawlers and river boats. Between 26 May and 4 June, 865 boats rescued 215,587 British soldiers and 127,031 French soldiers from Dunkirk (see Source 2).

This was an amazing achievement. Churchill had expected only a tenth of that number to be saved. Although they left behind them a huge amount of equipment, this meant that Britain still had an army.

Defending the island

After Dunkirk, Hitler thought that Britain was in no mood to fight. He offered to make peace on moderate terms. Churchill rejected the offer and chose to fight on. Hitler therefore ordered an invasion of Britain by air, sea and land forces.

Defending Britain against invasion was easier said than done. Germany had two hundred army divisions across the Channel. Britain had only twenty-seven divisions to fight them. Civilians were therefore asked to help defend Britain. Over a million men joined a defence force called the Home Guard. Source 3 shows some of the ways in which the Home Guard got ready to defend Britain.

The Battle of Britain

The first stage of the German invasion was carried out by the German air force. Its orders were to destroy the Royal Air Force (RAF). If it did this, British planes could not attack the ships bringing German soldiers across the Channel. Throughout the summer of 1940 German and British pilots fought each other in the 'Battle of Britain', high above southern England (see Source 4).

By the end of September the RAF was close to defeat. Its airfields were badly damaged, and it did not have enough pilots. On 7 September, however, the Germans stopped attacking the RAF's airfields and started bombing London instead. This was in revenge for British air raids on Berlin. It gave the RAF a chance to recover its strength and reorganise its forces.

A week later, flying in different formations, the RAF shot down sixty German aircraft on a bombing raid over London. From then on, the Germans stopped daytime bombing and went over to night-time bombing. This meant that the RAF had control of the air space over Britain. It could still attack any invasion force. Hitler was forced to cancel his invasion plans.

Source 3

This photograph was taken on 5 June 1940. It shows how people in a village in Northumberland made a roadblock with old carts, fences, railings, and other odds and ends from nearby farms.

Source 4

Fight over Portland, painted in the summer of 1940 by Richard Eurich, a British artist. He went to Portland, a British naval base on the Channel, every day during the Battle of Britain to paint this scene.

Questions

1 Look at Source 1.

a In your own words, say what Churchill was offering the British people.

b What would have been the alternative to this?

c This speech was very popular among the British people, despite what Churchill was offering them. Suggest why it was popular.

2 Look at Sources 2 and 4.

a Explain briefly the events that these paintings portray.

b How did each event help to save Britain from defeat?

c Which event do you think was the most important? Explain your answer.

Why did the war become global?

The war began in Europe in 1939. By the end of 1941 it had spread to Africa, Asia and the Pacific. Why did the war spread to the rest of the globe?

War in the Mediterranean

Mussolini, the Italian dictator, wanted to make Italy rich by capturing land around the Mediterranean. The British were determined to stop him. The Mediterranean was a vital shipping route between Britain and its oilfields in the Gulf (see Source 1).

In October 1940 the Italian army invaded Greece. The attack failed. The Greeks quickly drove them back. Soon after, British aircraft destroyed part of the Italian navy at Taranto. Mussolini was in trouble.

Mussolini's failure alarmed Hitler. He feared that the British would set up air bases in Greece and bomb the oil wells in Romania from which Germany got its oil. So Hitler decided to bring the whole region under his control. He put pressure on the countries there to become his allies. Hungary, Romania and Bulgaria agreed to do so, but Yugoslavia refused. So German forces invaded Yugoslavia and occupied it. They occupied Greece at the same time.

On the other side of the Mediterranean, there was fighting in North Africa. German and Italian troops tried to cut off Britain's oil supplies through the Suez Canal. After some early defeats they forced the British to retreat. By mid 1941 it looked as if they would soon take control of Egypt.

KEY

- land occupied by Germany
- land occupied by Italy
- German attacks
- Italian attacks
- British trade route
- British attacks

Source 1

The war spreads to the Mediterranean and the Soviet Union, 1940-41.

Germany conquers the Soviet Union

As you have read, Hitler and Stalin agreed in 1939 that they would not fight each other. This was not because they were friends but because it suited them both at the time. Hitler did not stop hating communism, and he did not stop wanting extra land. In June 1941 he broke the agreement and invaded the Soviet Union. The Soviet forces were unprepared for the attack. They had to retreat and give up huge areas of their country. By the end of 1941 the Germans had occupied a huge area of the western Soviet Union.

War in the Far East

War had started in the Far East in 1931, when the Japanese invaded Manchuria (see page 44). They invaded the rest of China in 1937. In 1941 they invaded French Indo-China and got ready to attack the East Indies and the Philippines.

Only Britain and the USA had the power to stop Japan doing this. But before either could act, the Japanese launched surprise attacks on their navy bases at Pearl Harbor and on Singapore. In these attacks, Britain and the USA lost so many warships that they could not stop the Japanese. Source 2 shows the huge area that Japan went on to conquer in the Pacific.

As a result of the attack on Pearl Harbor, the USA declared war on Japan on 8 December 1941. Germany and Italy, who had become allies of Japan a year earlier, then declared war on the USA. The war which had started in Europe thus spread to the other side of the globe to become a world war.

KEY

- Japanese land in 1930
- land captured by Japan 1931-41
- → Japanese attacks in December 1941
- ⬭ land under Japanese control by the end of 1942

Source 2

The spread of war in the Far East. This map, which is centred on the Pacific Ocean, shows how the Japanese conquered hundreds of Pacific islands as well as large parts of the Asian mainland.

Questions

1 a Put these events into the order in which they happened:
- Italy's invasion of Greece
- Japan's attack on the US navy base at Pearl Harbor
- the attack on Egypt by Italian and German forces.

b Explain how each event caused the war to spread beyond central Europe.

2 Suppose that Britain and Germany had their own oil in 1940, and did not need oil from Romania and the Gulf. Would the war have spread to the Mediterranean region? Explain your answer.

How were the Axis countries defeated?

By 1942 the world was split into two enemy alliances. On one side were Britain, the USA, the Soviet Union and twenty-three other countries. They were the Allies. On the other side were Germany, Italy, Japan and five other countries. They were known as the Axis countries.

Three turning points

Three important victories in 1942 and 1943 allowed the Allies to start winning back the land they had lost.

- In the Pacific Ocean the United States navy beat the Japanese navy at the Battle of Midway in June 1942 (see Source 1). Then they started to expel the Japanese from the Pacific islands which they had conquered.

- In Africa the British beat a German army at Alamein in November 1942. Then, with the Americans, they forced the Germans and Italians out of North Africa. They went on to invade Italy, forcing it to surrender in July 1943.

- In the Soviet Union, Soviet forces destroyed a German army after a five-month battle at Stalingrad (August 1942 to February 1943). Then they forced the other German armies in the Soviet Union to retreat.

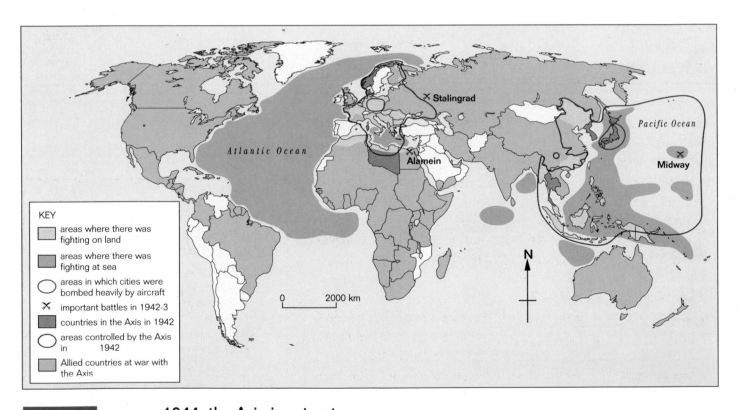

KEY

- areas where there was fighting on land
- areas where there was fighting at sea
- areas in which cities were bombed heavily by aircraft
- ✗ important battles in 1942-3
- countries in the Axis in 1942
- areas controlled by the Axis in 1942
- Allied countries at war with the Axis

Source 1

Global war, 1942-45.

1944: the Axis in retreat

By 1944 the Axis forces were retreating in every area of the fighting. Soviet forces pushed the Germans out of the Soviet Union, back into Europe. American and British forces invaded Normandy in France on D-Day in June. After heavy fighting they drove the Germans out of France. In the Pacific the Americans slowly forced the Japanese to leave the islands they had taken. Soon the Americans were close enough to Japan to bomb it from the air. In the Battle of the Atlantic, Allied warships destroyed large numbers of German submarines which had been attacking supply boats.

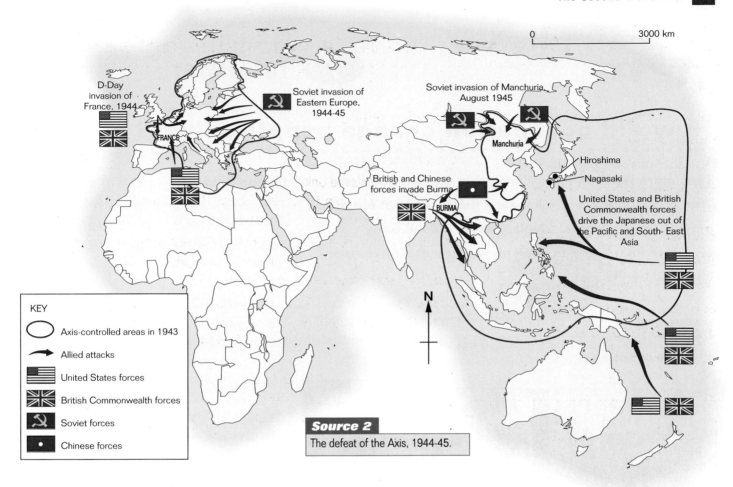

Source 2

The defeat of the Axis, 1944-45.

KEY

- Axis-controlled areas in 1943
- Allied attacks
- United States forces
- British Commonwealth forces
- Soviet forces
- Chinese forces

1945: the defeat of Germany

Early in 1945 the Allies closed in on Germany. Soviet forces drove the Germans out of eastern Europe and back into Germany. British and American forces invaded from the west after forcing the Germans out of France, Belgium and Holland. By May 1945 they had control of the whole country. When they entered the capital, Berlin, Hitler committed suicide. A new government surrendered to the Allies a week later.

1945: the defeat of Japan

The war against Japan went on for another fourteen weeks. Japanese soldiers fought with incredible determination to stop the Allies from advancing. They fought the British in Burma, the Americans in the Pacific, the Soviets in Manchuria, and the Chinese in China. It looked as if the Allies would have to invade Japan and fight a land war to force the Japanese to surrender.

This did not happen because, in August 1945, the US Air Force dropped two atomic bombs on the cities of Hiroshima and Nagasaki. These newly-developed bombs were a thousand times more powerful than any other bomb which then existed. The two cities were destroyed and 150,000 people were killed. Fearing that the Americans would drop more atomic bombs, the Japanese emperor surrendered on 15 August 1945. The Second World War was over.

Questions

1 Look carefully at Source 1, then decide which of these statements are true and which are false.

- Most countries of the world were involved in the Second World War.
- Fighting took place on land, at sea, and in the air.
- Most of the fighting took place in Europe.
- The Axis countries outnumbered the Allied countries.

2 a Read the text on these pages, then put these events into the order in which they happened:

- the Battle of Stalingrad
- the Battle of Midway
- the D-Day invasion of France
- the Battle of Alamein.

b Why was each of these battles important in changing the course of the war?

7 Total war

How did occupation change people's lives?

Even more than the First World War, the Second World War was a total war. This means that it was not fought only by armed forces. Civilians were also directly involved. Part 7 of this book shows how their lives were changed by the war.

Occupation

The Germans and the Japanese occupied each of the countries they conquered. This meant that 770 million people in thirty countries came under their rule. Source 1 shows just a handful of them.

Occupation involved three things. First, the occupiers took over the government and imposed their laws on the people. Second, they kept large armies in the countries they occupied to prevent rebellions against them. Third, they plundered the countries of food, materials and machinery. Sources 2 and 3 tell you more about these aspects of occupation.

Source 1

The only part of the United Kingdom occupied by Germany was the Channel Islands. This photograph shows a German army band playing at St Helier on the island of Jersey.

Source 3

Part of an order that the Germans intended to issue after invading Britain in 1940.

Directive for military government in England.

1 The main task of military government is to make full use of the country's resources for the needs of the fighting troops and the requirements of the German war economy.

2 An essential condition for securing the labour of the country is that law and order should prevail. Law and order will therefore be established....

3 Armed rebels of either sex will be treated with the utmost severity....

4 The able-bodied male population between the ages of 17 and 45 will be interned (*imprisoned*) and despatched to the continent....

Source 2

From an anonymous letter written by a Czech in 1940.

Foreign occupation changes every detail of your life.... You cannot get proper food. It is not the rationing itself which brings discomfort but rather the way your food is rationed and why.... Your restriction is not a necessary sacrifice which you are making for your country... You are starving in order that the men you hate should be well fed.... Your mother or your wife must stand with their food cards in long queues before the shops... supervised by the German police. You are cold at home because you cannot get any coal.... You cannot wash your hands because there is no soap.

Resistance

In every occupied country, people resisted the rule of the Germans and Japanese. The simplest way of doing this was by refusing to co-operate with them. For example, many French people pretended not to understand orders given to them in German. Dutch people got up and left when German soldiers entered their cafés. Indonesians avoided saluting the Japanese flag. More dangerously, several million men and women took part in armed resistance. They used sabotage and murder against the occupiers (see Source 4).

Repression

Both the Germans and Japanese dealt harshly with resisters. In German-held countries, this was done by the Gestapo, the Nazi secret police. Source 5 gives us an idea of their methods.

Source 5

A poster put up on walls in the French city of Nantes in 1941.

Cowardly criminals in the pay of England and Moscow have killed, by shooting in the back, the Field Commander of Nantes on the morning of 20 October 1941. In payment for this crime I have already ordered that fifty hostages be shot.... Fifty more hostages will be shot if the guilty parties are not arrested by midnight, 23 October. I offer a reward of 15 million francs to citizens who contribute towards the discovery of the guilty parties.

Source 4

This poster shows ten French Resistance fighters executed in 1944. Put up all over France by the Germans, the poster says 'Freedom fighters? Liberation by an army of criminals!' The pictures show their 'crimes' - blowing up railway lines and shooting German soldiers.

Questions

1   a Source 2 describes three ways in which occupation made life uncomfortable. What were they?

      b The writer of Source 2 was not complaining only about discomfort. What was his main complaint?

2   Read Source 3. If the Germans had occupied Britain in 1940, how would the lives of many British people have been changed?

3   Read Source 5.

      a What is a hostage?

      b Suppose that somebody who saw the killing of the German Commander read this poster in 1941. Why might he or she want to tell the German police about it?

      c Nobody did give information to the police about the killing, and the hostages were all shot. Suggest why nobody came forward to the police.

4   a What impression does Source 1 create of the occupation of a country?

      b Judging by the information and Sources on these pages, explain how accurate you think that impression is.

Why did some people collaborate?

As you have read, the Germans and Japanese ruled the countries they had occupied harshly. Some people opposed this by joining Resistance groups. But just as many helped the occupiers. They were known as collaborators. What made people collaborate?

Source 1

An eye-witness describes how the Gestapo, helped by a gang of criminals, punished the people of a town after a local resistance group killed two German officers.

> The brutes break into houses, smash furniture, steal silver, jewellery, clocks and family treasures, and seize provisions. They eat children's chocolates and drink wine and spirits.... Vans go up and down the streets collecting clothes, bedding, crockery and silver....
>
> A bus full of men arrives. They are resisters who have been arrested by the Gestapo.... These 25 have been chosen to pay with their lives for the killing of the two German officers.... The Bonny-Lafont men *(the gang)* come running out of the houses.... They take the prisoners to the 'Black Fountains' and shoot them.

The 'economic collaborators'

Many people helped the occupiers because their jobs made it difficult not to do so. For example, many police and local government officials helped them keep law and order. Shopkeepers, traders and bankers did business with them because their livelihoods depended on it.

Some went further than this. There was a great deal of money to be made through 'economic collaboration'. Conquered countries had to pay the costs of the occupying army. France, for example, had to pay 400 million francs a day to maintain the German army there. The German army spent this money buying huge quantities of goods: whole boatloads of grain, entire herds of cattle, thousands of litres of wine. Some farmers and businessmen collaborated with the Germans in order to win these valuable contracts.

The most extreme form of 'economic collaboration' was by criminal gangs. In France, some helped the Gestapo to hunt down resisters because, in return, the Gestapo ignored their crimes. Source 1 is an example of this.

Hating the enemy's enemy

Some people collaborated because they did not hate their enemy as much as they hated their own country's allies. Many of the French saw the British as a greater enemy than the Germans. This was partly because the British and French had been enemies in many wars throughout history. Source 2 illustrates this. It was also partly because of things the British had done to France during the war. For example, many believed that the British had deliberately left 40,000 French soldiers behind at Dunkirk in 1940 (see Source 3).

Source 2

A poster which French collaborators put up in 1944 on the anniversary of Jeanne d'Arc's death. Jeanne led an army against the English during the Hundred Years War. The English burned her to death after capturing her in 1431.

1412	Jeanne is born at Donremy.
1429	Jeanne defeats the English at Orléans.
1430	Jeanne is taken prisoner at Compiègne.
1431	Jeanne is burnt alive at Rouen, BY THE ENGLISH.
1939	France is dragged into the war BY THE ENGLISH.
1940	France is betrayed at Dunkirk ... BY THE ENGLISH.
1942	France is stripped of its colonies BY THE ENGLISH.
1944	French towns are bombed every day BY THE ENGLISH.

Source 3

This French poster says '1940 - Dunkirk. The English stop the last of the French, who came to protect their retreat, from getting on the boats'.

1940. DUNKERQUE LES ANGLAIS S'OPPOSENT A L'EMBARQUEMENT DES DERNIERS FRANÇAIS QUI VENAIENT DE PROTEGER LEUR RETRAITE

'Horizontal collaborators'

In many places, young women became friendly with German soldiers. For some, it was a way of getting hold of things in short supply: German soldiers could supply them with cigarettes, sweets, or nylon stockings, for example. For others, it was the result of physical attraction. Many had sexual relations with German soldiers. In France, they were known as 'horizontal collaborators'.

The punishment of collaborators

Understandably, the resisters hated the collaborators. When the war ended in 1945 they took revenge. In France they secretly executed around 30,000 collaborators without trials. Thousands of men were beaten up by angry mobs. And in scenes like the one below (Source 4), thousands of women had their heads shaved bare for being 'horizontal collaborators'.

Source 4

After the Germans had left France in 1944, 'horizontal collaborators' like these women had their heads shaved and were paraded in public.

Questions

1. What reasons for collaboration can you find in Sources 2 and 3?

2. How do those reasons differ from the reasons of the gang in Source 1?

3. Look at Source 4.

   a. The bystanders appear to have been enjoying themselves. Why do you think that was?

   b. What might the women have been feeling about what was happening to them?

   c. What might they have said in defence of their actions as collaborators?

4. Can any of the reasons for collaboration be excused? Explain your answer.

Why were civilians bombed?

In Britain, Germany and Japan, civilians in big towns and cities were regularly bombed by enemy aircraft. Why was this done, and what were the results?

Bombers and their targets

When the war began, both sides tried using 'precision bombing' to hit targets such as ports, factories or railway junctions. The aim was to destroy the enemy's trade and industry, making it impossible for them to fight. Source 1 shows some of the targets of British bombers.

Precision bombing did not work. Bombs often did not hit their targets. When they did, the damage was not always severe. Both sides therefore started bombing whole towns and cities rather than just military or industrial targets. The British called this 'area bombing'.

Effects of area bombing

Area bombing caused huge destruction. American and British planes dropped 2,697,473 tonnes of bombs on 131 German cities. They killed 800,000 people and made 7.5 million homeless. Source 2 shows that the British were trying not only to destroy German industry but also the Germans' will to fight.

Some bombing raids were so heavy that they created firestorms. In a firestorm, the hot air which rises from burning buildings is replaced by cooler air rushing in from outside the buildings. This becomes a hurricane-force wind which superheats the fire. Sources 3 and 4 give an idea of the firestorm that took place in Hamburg in 1943.

Source 2

Advice given to the British government in 1942 by Lord Cherwell, a senior scientific adviser.

In 1938 over 22 million Germans lived in fifty-eight towns of over 100,000 inhabitants. If even half our bombs were dropped on ... these fifty-eight towns the great majority of their inhabitants (about one third of the German population) would be turned out of house and home. Investigation seems to show that having one's home demolished is most damaging to morale.... There seems little doubt that this would break the spirit of the people.

Source 3

A report written by Hamburg's police chief on the firestorm in Hamburg in summer 1943.

People jumped into the canals and waterways and remained swimming or standing up to their necks in water for hours until the heat died down. Even these suffered burns on their heads.... The firestorm swept over the water with its ... showers of sparks so that even thick wooden posts burned down to the level of the water.... Children were torn away from their parents' hands by the force of the hurricane and whirled into the fire.

Source 4

A street in Hamburg after the firestorm of July 1943. These people died when fires burning at 1000°C used up so much oxygen that they suffocated.

Source 5

Sir Arthur Harris, chief of Bomber Command, writing in his memoirs in 1947.

In spite of all that happened at Hamburg, bombing proved a comparatively humane method. For one thing, it saved the youth of this country and of our allies from being mown down by the military, as it was in ... the war of 1914-1918.

Source 6

From the report of the British Bombing Survey Unit set up at the end of the war to study the effects of area bombing on Germany.

Huge areas in many towns all over Germany were severely stricken and some were devastated, but the ... effect on war production was remarkably small.... The German war economy was more resilient than estimated.... The will of the German people was not broken, nor even significantly impaired.... The German people proved calmer, more stoical and much more determined than anticipated.

Was area bombing necessary?

Did this terrible destruction help the Allies to win the war? The man who organised the bombing, Sir Arthur Harris, was sure that it was (see Source 5). But when the war was over, researchers questioned whether the bombing had achieved its aims (see Source 6).

At the end of the war, the British government did not honour the airmen who bombed Germany. They received no campaign medals. Sir Arthur Harris was not in the Victory Honours list. For forty-seven years, he was the only war commander not to have an official statue made of him. When, in 1992, a statue of 'Bomber Harris' was unveiled in London, protesters threw paint at it (see Source 7).

Source 7

The statue of Sir Arthur Harris, put up in London in 1992.

Questions

1 Look at Source 1 carefully.

  a Make a list of at least five kinds of target attacked by British bombers.

  b For each kind of target, say how bombing it could help to win the war.

2 a What different reason for bombing is given in Source 2?

  b Why, according to Source 6, was Lord Cherwell wrong?

3 Sir Arthur Harris said (Source 5) that bombing was a comparatively 'humane' method of warfare.

  a What does 'humane' mean?

  b What aspects of the 1914-18 war do you think Sir Arthur Harris had in mind when he said this?

  c Do Sources 3 and 4 agree with his point of view? Explain your answer.

4 Look at Source 7. Many people protested against this statue being put up. What points might a) a protester b) a supporter have made in a letter to a newspaper?

Displaced people

Having a home is a basic human need. Being homeless is a disaster for anyone. Many millions of people suffered that disaster during the Second World War. Why were so many people displaced from their homes, and how did this affect them?

Refugees

In every country where there was fighting, terrified people left their homes to seek refuge in safer places. Such people are known as refugees. The biggest movement of refugees took place at the end of the war in 1945. Sixteen million Germans lived in the occupied countries of eastern Europe. As the Soviet army advanced across Europe (see page 69) many of them fled in panic. They were terrified by thoughts of what the Soviet troops would do to them. Source 1 shows just a few of them. Out of 16 million refugees in 1945, about 3 million died of cold, hunger, disease and starvation.

Source 1

A family of German refugees in Berlin at the end of the war in 1945.

Source 2

Two families of evacuees arriving in Eastbourne on 1 September 1939. As well as their luggage they are carrying gas-masks in cardboard boxes around their necks. The labels they are wearing are name tags.

Evacuees

In several countries, the government took large numbers of civilians from their city homes to live with families in countryside areas. This was to protect them from air raids by enemy bombers. It was known as evacuation.

In Britain, evacuation began on 1 September 1939. Around 1.5 million women and children were taken, mostly by train, to towns and villages all over the country (see Source 2). But the expected air raids did not take place. And, as Source 3 suggests, evacuation could be an unpleasant experience. Within six months, most evacuees had returned to their homes in the cities.

Deportees

Millions of people in the occupied countries were taken from their homes to work for the occupying forces. Over a million Chinese and Koreans were sent to Japan to work on farms and in mines and factories. Many thousands of Korean women were forced to be prostitutes for Japanese soldiers. In occupied Europe, 3.5 million Poles and Russians were sent to Germany to do slave labour. Source 4 gives us an idea of the life these people led.

It wasn't only in the occupied countries that people were deported from their homes. In the Allied countries, people with foreign backgrounds were put in prison camps so that they could not help the enemy in an invasion. In Britain, for example, people of German and Italian origin were kept in camps until the end of the war.

Most deportations took place in the Soviet Union. The Soviet government did not trust the non-Russian peoples to stay loyal. It sent 400,000 German-speaking people from the Volga region to prison camps in distant Siberia, and a million non-Russians from the Black Sea area to Central Asia.

Source 3

Mary Baxter, aged 11 in 1939, recalling her evacuation experiences in an interview in 1988.

I was placed in a workman's cottage and woke up the first morning to the screams of a pig. I looked out of the window and saw several people beating the animal with sticks and there was a horny-handed yokel cutting the pig's throat at the same time. It was their method of killing pigs....

The foster mum thought she was onto a very good thing with me and the other eleven-year-old girl billeted with her. I think she regarded it as a business transaction. We were expected to shop and wash up and look after a whining three-year-old....

Source 4

A government order of 1943 telling German farmers how to treat Polish farmworkers.

1 Polish farmworkers no longer have the right to complain.
2 Polish farmworkers may not leave the areas in which they are employed.
3 The use of bicycles is strictly prohibited.
4 Visiting churches, regardless of faith, is strictly prohibited.
5 Visits to theatres, cinemas or other entertainments are strictly prohibited.
6 Visiting restaurants is strictly prohibited.
7 Sexual intercourse with women and girls is strictly prohibited.
8 Gatherings of Polish farmworkers after work are prohibited.
9 The use of railways, buses and other public conveyances is strictly prohibited.
10 Polish farmworkers have to work daily for as long as the employer demands.
11 Every employer has the right to beat Polish farmworkers.

Questions

1 Compare Sources 1 and 2.
  a Which picture shows refugees, and which shows evacuees?
  b What is the difference between a refugee and an evacuee?

2 Look at Source 4.
  a People in democratic countries have human and civil rights (see page 42). What rights were taken away from Polish workers by this government order?
  b Suggest why the Germans deprived Polish workers of so many rights.

3 a Use the sources and information on these pages to make a list of things that were bad about each of the following: being evacuated; being deported; being a refugee.
  b Which do you consider to be worst? Explain your answer.

Thought control

In every country at war, governments did all they could to control the way people thought about the war. Why did they do this, and what methods did they use?

Propaganda

All governments spent a great deal of money on propaganda. Propaganda is a form of advertising. Its aim is to persuade people to believe certain things, usually to do with politics. Propaganda can be visual, using film, television or posters. It can be printed in newspapers, magazines and leaflets. Or it can be spoken, in radio broadcasts or speeches. The most common form of propaganda during the war was the wall poster. Posters like Sources 1 and 2 were cheap to produce, and they put across messages simply and quickly.

Very few people had television during the war, but most had a radio. This meant that each country could transmit propaganda directly into the homes of people in enemy countries. Britain, for example, broadcast programmes in forty-seven languages to occupied countries and to Germany. Source 3 is an example of a programme broadcast to Germany.

Source 1

A British poster of 1942 shows a shepherd and his dog bringing in sheep on the South Downs in Sussex

your BRITAIN · fight for it now

ISSUED BY A·B·C·A

Source 3

A 'special announcement' broadcast in German to western Germany in 1945, by a British radio transmitter. The announcer was pretending to be a senior Nazi official.

Comrades! The enemy has reached the gates of our district!... Our people are open to all the effects of modern weapons and threatened with complete destruction.... Our evacuation plans have become impossible, so only people who are able to continue fighting will be evacuated. The evacuation of most citizens will, for the time being, be impossible. Their duty, therefore, is to stick it out and, if need be, to face death bravely.

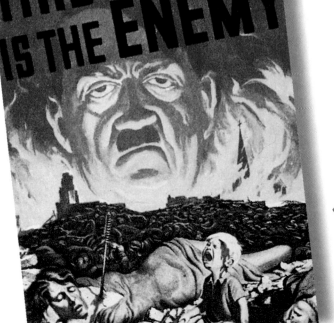

THIS IS THE ENEMY

Source 2

This American poster of 1942 shows a weeping child and his dead parents in the wreckage of their home, with the face of Hitler in the background.

Source 4

This bogus letter was supposed to have been written by the friend of a dead German soldier to the soldier's family. It was actually written by Britain's Political Warfare Executive.

Dear Frau Müller

They have probably told you that your Heinz died from jaundice. That was not the case. We were in the same Company and he was a fine chap. They had to amputate his leg and afterwards gave him a lethal injection. This often happens to war cripples. I'll visit you after the war.

Source 5

Members of the Women's Voluntary Service collect aluminium cooking pans for conversion into war planes, in Sidcup in 1942.

Misinformation

Propaganda sometimes took the form of lies. 'Whisper propaganda', for example, involved the spreading of false rumours and wrong information. One way of doing this was by sending forged letters like the one shown in Source 4 to people in enemy countries. In Britain this was organised by a group called the Political Warfare Executive.

Censorship

Another method of controlling people's thoughts was censorship. In every country, officials called censors checked printed materials, films and photographs. Their job was to make sure that these did not contain anything which might help the enemy, or damage the country's war effort. In Britain, for example, the Censorship Bureau banned all press photographs which showed dead air-raid victims or houses destroyed by bombs.

Rallies and campaigns

In every country at war, people were encouraged to join campaigns to help the war effort. Campaigns to recycle materials were especially popular. In Britain, for example, housewives were asked to give in their aluminium pans to help make aircraft (see Source 5). However, it was expensive and difficult to recycle the pans, and many were simply thrown away. Even so, such campaigns made people feel they were giving something valuable to the war effort. This helped to boost their morale.

Questions

1 Look at Sources 1 and 2.
   a What do you think each poster was trying to persuade people to think?
   b What different methods did the artists use to achieve this?

2 Look at Sources 3 and 4.
   a What feelings might the people who received these messages have had?
   b What effect do you think the Political Warfare Executive hoped to achieve with these messages?
   c Which do you think was most likely to succeed in creating this effect?

3 Very few of the cooking pans collected during the war were made into aircraft. Does this mean that the campaign shown in Source 5 was totally pointless?

Economies at war

Victory in the war depended not only on which side had the strongest army. It depended also on which side had the strongest economy. What is an 'economy', and why were countries' economies so important in the Second World War?

Economies

We use the word economy to describe everything that is concerned with making, buying and selling things. A country's industry, agriculture, trade, money and commerce are all parts of its economy. A country with a strong economy produces many goods, sells to other countries more than it buys from them, and provides its people with a good standard of living.

The war boosts production

Wars use up huge amounts of materials and equipment. A bomb cannot be remade once it has exploded. A crashed plane cannot be rebuilt. A sunken warship stays at the bottom of the sea. Yet while the war goes on, all these must be replaced if the armies are to continue fighting. Between 1939 and 1945, therefore, vast quantities of metal, chemicals, rubber, glass and hundreds of other materials were constantly being destroyed and replaced. Source 1 gives an idea of the materials needed for just one warplane.

Source 1

This painting shows how an American B-29 'Superfortress' bomber was constructed. The B-29 was the largest bomber made in the Second World War.

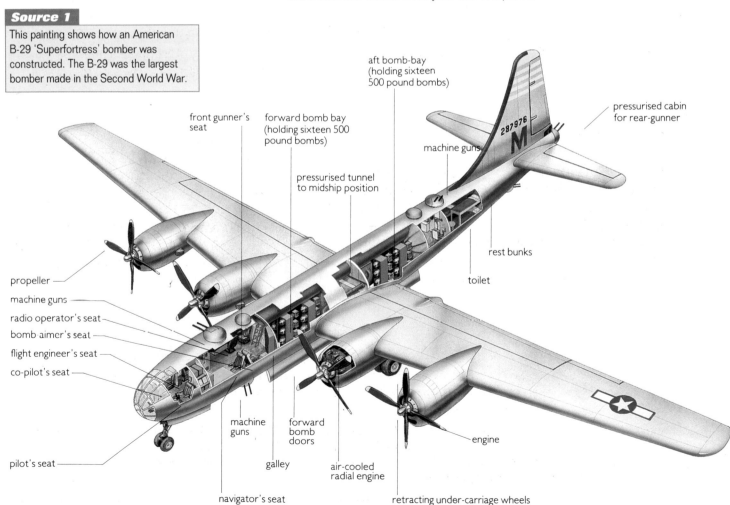

aft bomb-bay
(holding sixteen
500 pound bombs)

pressurised cabin
for rear-gunner

front gunner's
seat

forward bomb bay
(holding sixteen 500
pound bombs)

machine guns

pressurised tunnel
to midship position

rest bunks

toilet

propeller

machine guns

radio operator's seat

bomb aimer's seat

flight engineer's seat

co-pilot's seat

machine
guns

forward
bomb
doors

engine

pilot's seat

galley

air-cooled
radial engine

navigator's seat

retracting under-carriage wheels

Source 2

A US poster encouraging war production.

Source 2

A US poster encouraging war production.

The American economy at war

The country which produced the greatest amount of war materials was the United States of America. The USA had huge reserves of raw materials and energy, and was soon providing war materials for its allies as well as for itself. Between 1940 and 1945, workers in the USA made more than 300,000 war planes, 96,000 tanks, 61,000 heavy guns, seven million rifles, two million lorries, and all the other things soldiers need for warfare. Source 2 reflects the importance of workers in the American war effort.

The Soviet economy at war

The Soviet Union was almost defeated when the Germans invaded in 1941 (see page 66). One reason why it survived was that the Soviets moved their biggest factories out of the Germans' reach. They took the machines and buildings of 1,523 factories to pieces, put them into a million train-loads, and took them to the east of the country. Source 3 describes how steel workers from the Ukraine rebuilt their factory in the Ural mountains.

Source 3

A description of how steel workers rebuilt their factory in the Ural mountains.

Source 4

From *The Memoirs of Marshal Zhukov*, the Soviet Union's leading general in the war.

They were given seventy-five days, from the end of December 1941 to mid-March 1942. They had to re-establish seven main and eleven auxiliary production shops together with railway lines, water supplies, air shafts; all this in 45 degrees of frost, with the soil frozen to a depth of two metres. They had to heat the ground, drill it and break it up with explosives, keep the concrete from freezing, working round the clock…. The job was finished ahead of schedule, in six weeks.

The heroic feat of the evacuation and rebuilding of industry during the war meant as much for the country's destiny as the greatest battles of the war.

Questions

1   a   Ask your teacher for Copymaster 29 and complete it, following the instructions.

     b   Look at your completed copymaster. How do you think wartime aircraft building changed (a) the output of factories, (b) the employment of workers, and (c) company profits?

2   Read Sources 3 and 4.

     a   Marshal Zhukov said (Source 4) that the rebuilding of industry was 'a heroic feat'. Why might the rebuilding of the factory described in Source 3 be called 'heroic'?

     b   Why do you think Marshal Zhukov thought this rebuilding was just as important as the greatest battles of the war?

The Holocaust

As you have read (on page 59) the Nazis started treating Jewish people badly when they came to power in Germany. This bad treatment quickly turned to violence and then to mass murder. Between 1939 and 1945 the Nazis murdered nearly six million Jewish people. How was such an appalling crime possible?

Source 1
This poster shows the kinds of men Nazis thought belonged to the Aryan race: 'Nordic', 'Falian', 'Eastern Baltic', 'Western', 'Dinaric', and 'Eastern'.

Source 2
Laws against Jews made between 1938 and 1941.

Decree regarding the change of family names, 17 August 1938.
Jews are allowed certain first names only.... Jews with first names different from those listed must use the first name 'Israel' (for men) and 'Sara' (for women) in addition to their own names.

Order by the Reich Minister for Education, 16 November 1938.
Jews may only attend Jewish schools. All Jewish students not yet dismissed from German schools must be dismissed immediately.

Decree by the Berlin police, 3 December 1938.
Jews are banned from all cinemas, shows, concert and lecture halls, museums, amusement places, sports fields....

Decree regarding identification badges for Jews, 1 September 1941.
Jews over six years of age must wear the 'Star of David' when in public. The 'Star of David' is a black, six-pointed star on yellow material...with the inscription 'Jew'.

Nazi race theories

Nazis believed that all human beings belonged to different races and that some races were superior to others. In Nazi eyes, the Germans were Aryans, who Nazis believed were a 'master race' (see Source 1). They wanted to keep the Aryan race 'pure' by staying apart from other races, especially Jews.

Nazi laws against Jews

They began by making laws to keep Jews apart from Aryans. As you have read (Source 6, page 59) the first of these laws said that Jews could not be German citizens or marry German citizens. Further laws took away the rights of Jews and restricted their opportunities (see Source 2).

The encouragement of racial hatred

Making laws against Jews was only one way of restricting them. The Nazis also put a lot of effort into changing people's behaviour towards Jews. Young people especially were encouraged to hate Jews. School lessons put across anti-semitic - or anti-Jewish - views (see Sources 3 and 4). This was accompanied by a big increase in the bullying of Jewish children (see Source 5).

Organised violence against Jews

Jews often tried to resist the Nazis, but this could result in even worse treatment. In November 1938, for example, a Jew shot dead a Nazi official. In reprisal, armed Nazis organised a campaign of terror against the Jewish population. They called it 'The Night of Broken Glass'. Ten thousand shopkeepers had their shop windows smashed and the contents stolen. Ninety-one Jews were murdered and 20,000 were thrown into concentration camps.

Ghettoes

During the war, Jews in countries occupied by the Germans also began to suffer. In Poland, for example, Jews were made to live in ghettoes. A ghetto was a walled-off area of a town or city which the inhabitants were not allowed to leave. In Warsaw, which was a city of 1,200,000 people, 400,000 Jews were made to live in an area one fiftieth the size of the city. Walled into this tiny area, with no means of escape, tens of thousands of Jews starved to death.

Source 3

A homework exercise given to German schoolchildren to learn.

1. The Jewish race is much inferior to the Negro race.
2. All Jews have crooked legs, fat bellies, curly hair and a suspicious look.
3. The Jews were responsible for the World War.
4. They are to blame for the armistice of 1918 and the Versailles treaty.
5. They caused the Inflation.
6. They brought about the downfall of the Roman Empire.
7. Marx is a great criminal.
8. All Jews are Communists....

Source 4

In this German classroom in 1935, two Jewish boys have been made to stand in front of the class during a lesson about Jews. The writing on the board says 'The Jews are our greatest enemy! Beware of the Jews!' The star on the board is the Star of David, a symbol of the Jewish religion.

Source 5

An extract from the diary of a German journalist living in Nazi Germany.

June 1, 1938
Driving out to Potsdam, I came across a group of youngsters, dressed in the Hitler Youth outfit, beating up a skinny, undersized, fair-haired boy. I stopped!

'Aren't you ashamed, eight big strong fellows like you, jumping on a six-year-old kid?'

The oldest of the gang explained. 'We discovered that this dirty little swine was nothing but a Jewish bastard. He refused to answer the *Heil Hitler* salute, and said he was Jewish....

I took the trembling child home to his parents.

Questions

1. Describe how a Jewish person's life in Germany might have been changed by the laws in Source 2.

2. Work in a group of three. Each choose one of Sources 1,2 and 3. Prepare a one-minute talk in which you tell the others how this material might have encouraged people in Germany to treat Jews badly.

3. How can you explain the behaviour of the boys described in Source 5?

Source 6

This picture was painted by a former prisoner in Auschwitz extermination camp. It shows women at Auschwitz being taken to be killed in a gas chamber.

Source 7

A former Nazi officer in Belzec extermination camp describes what happened to Jews selected to die. He was giving evidence in a trial of Nazi war criminals at the end of the war.

A loudspeaker gave instructions: 'Strip, even artificial limbs and glasses. Hand all money and valuables in at the 'valuables' window. Women and young girls are to have their hair cut in the 'barber's hut'...'

Stark naked men, women, children and cripples passed by.... SS men pushed them into the gas chambers. 'Fill it up', Wirth ordered. Seven to eight hundred people in ninety-three square metres.... All were dead after thirty-two minutes.

Jewish workers on the other side opened the wooden doors. They had been promised their lives in return for doing this horrible work.... The people were still standing like columns of stone, with no room to fall or lean. Even in death you could tell the families, all holding hands. It was difficult to separate them while emptying out the room for the next batch. The bodies were tossed out.... Two dozen workers were busy checking mouths which they opened with iron hooks.... Dentists knocked out gold teeth, bridges and crowns with hammers.

Captain Wirth stood in the middle of them...and, showing me a big jam box filled with teeth, said, 'See the weight of the gold! Just from yesterday and the day before!

Mass murder in the Soviet Union

Nearly three million Jews lived in the western part of the Soviet Union. When the Germans invaded in 1941, 'Special Action Groups' of soldiers followed them into the areas they occupied. Their orders were to kill the Jews in every town and village. They carried out their orders with dreadful efficiency. Whole communities of Jews were rounded up, and shot into mass graves.

The 'Final Solution'

In 1942, when most of Europe was under German rule, the Nazi leaders decided to carry out what they called 'the final solution' to the Jewish problem. By this they meant the killing of every Jew in Europe, either by murder or by working them to death.

To kill an estimated eleven million Jews, the Nazis set up 'extermination camps' in remote areas of Poland. Each camp was linked to the rest of Europe by rail. Jews were taken to the camps in long goods trains that ferried backwards and forwards across Europe. As soon as a train arrived at a camp, the passengers were divided into two groups: those who were to work and those who were to die. Sources 6 and 7 show us what happened to the second group. Source 8 explains why it was usually impossible for them to protect themselves from this fate.

Source 8

Primo Levi, an Italian Jew who was selected to work at Auschwitz camp, explains why most prisoners did not try to escape.

In most cases the new arrivals did not know what awaited them. They were received with cold efficiency but without brutality, invited to undress 'for the showers'. Sometimes they were handed soap and towels and promised hot coffee after their showers. The gas chambers were, in fact, camouflaged as shower rooms, with pipes, faucets, dressing rooms, clothes hooks, benches and so forth. When, instead, prisoners showed the smallest signs of suspecting their fate, the SS and their collaborators used ... extreme brutality, with shouts, threats, kicks, shots, loosing their dogs, which were trained to tear prisoners to pieces, against people who were often confused, desperate, weakened by five or ten days of travelling in sealed railroad cars.

KEY

☐ extermination camps

○ main concentration camps

➜ advance of the Special Action Groups

▬ Greater Germany, 1942

000 estimated minimum number of Jews murdered from each country

• mass murders carried out by the Special Action Groups

FINLAND **11**

NORWAY **728**

ESTONIA **1,000**

LATVIA **80,000**

DENMARK **77**

LITHUANIA **135,000**

HOLLAND **106,000**

BELGIUM **24,387**

Belsen

GERMANY **160,000**

SOVIET UNION **1,000,000**

P O L A N D

Chelmno **3,000,000**

Treblinka

Sobibor

Majdanek

Belzec

Auschwitz

LUXEMBOURG **700**

Dachau

C Z E C H O S L O V A K I A **217,000**

FRANCE **83,000**

AUSTRIA **65,000**

HUNGARY **365,000**

ITALY **8,000**

ROMANIA **364,632**

YUGOSLAVIA **60,000**

BULGARIA

0 — 500 km

ALBANIA **200**

GREECE **66,300**

Source 9

The Holocaust, 1939-45.

Questions

1
  a Look at Source 9. How many Jews were killed in the Holocaust?
  b Which five countries suffered the greatest loss of Jews in the Holocaust?

2 Look at Sources 6, 7 and 8.

  a In your own words, explain what happened to Jewish prisoners in the extermination camps.
  b Why was it difficult for Jews to prevent this happening to them?

3 Using all the Sources and information on pages 82 to 85, explain why you think it was possible for the Holocaust to happen.

Were the atomic bombs necessary?

On 6 August 1945 an American plane dropped a new kind of bomb on the city of Hiroshima in Japan. This atomic bomb killed 78,000 people and injured 40,000. A second atomic bomb exploded above the city of Nagasaki three days later, killing 40,000 people. Within a week, the Japanese surrendered, and the Second World War came to an end. As the Sources on these pages show, the atomic bombs had horrible effects. Was it really necessary to use them to make Japan surrender?

Effects of the atomic bomb

The atomic bomb exploded with a gigantic flash 570 metres above the city of Hiroshima. The heat was so intense that people nearest the flash evaporated, leaving only their shadows on the ground. Tens of thousands were turned into charred corpses. Many who survived were very badly burned. Even more died later from radiation poisoning. Sources 1 to 4 help us to imagine what it was like to be in Hiroshima on that day.

Source 1

This photograph was taken in Hiroshima two hours after the atomic bomb exploded over the city centre three kilometres away.

Source 2

This photograph of a test explosion on 25 July 1946 shows the awesome power of an atomic bomb. Disused warships were moored in the area to see what would happen to them. They were all destroyed.

Source 3

The centre of Hiroshima, photographed several weeks after the atomic bomb exploded above it.

Source 4

These paintings are by Tomoko Konishi, a survivor of the Hiroshima bomb. She did them in 1975 after seeing a television programme which asked survivors to draw or paint their memories. Along with hundreds of other survivors, she painted her memories so that future generations would not forget what had happened. The captions under each picture summarise what the Japanese writing says.

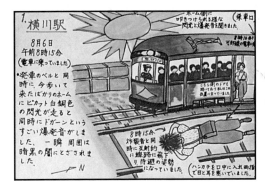

August 6. 1945. I got on a streetcar about 8.10 a.m. As I heard the starting bell ring I saw a silver flash and heard an explosion. Next moment everything went dark. Instinctively I jumped down on the track and braced myself.

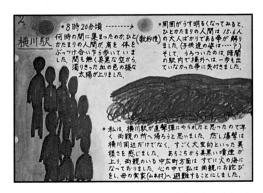

About 8.20 a.m. Soon the sun appeared blood red in the dark sky. Smoke was rising here and there. Nakahiro-cho where my parents lived was in flames. Apologising in my heart to my parents I decided to seek shelter.

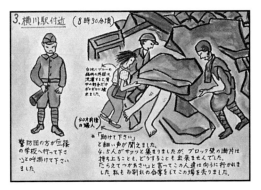

Around Yokogawa station about 8.30 a.m. I heard a woman saying in a small voice 'Please help me.' Four or five people got together to help her. But we couldn't lift the concrete block off her. Saying 'Forgive us' the others left her as she was. I prayed for her and then also left.

About 8.50 a.m. A lady about 40 years old was bleeding from her eyes. Unconsciously I wiped my face with my hands and I was surprised to see blood on them. I got my mirror out and looked into it. I found only a small cut on my eyebrow.

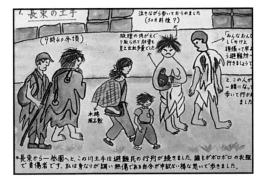

About 9.40 a.m. Refugees walked along the bank of the river. Everyone was in rags and hurt. A woman was crying 'Can anyone help me?' The flesh of her side was scooped out and bleeding and I could see her ribs.

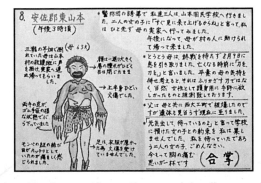

My mother. Her face was larger than usual, her lips were badly swollen. The skin of both her hands was hanging loose. The upper part of her body was badly burned. She passed away on August 9 before seeing the war end. My father disappeared and we never found the body.

Was there an alternative to the atomic bombs?

Ever since Hiroshima and Nagasaki were destroyed, people have argued about whether it was necessary to use atomic bombs. Some say that it was the only way of defeating Japan. They argue that the alternative was for Allied forces to invade Japan and to fight the Japanese army in battle. Sources 5, 6 and 7 show what this might have involved. An invasion would not only have killed huge numbers of soldiers but would also have put at risk prisoners of war being held by the Japanese (see Source 8).

Just as many people hold a different view. They say that Japan was close to defeat in 1945, and could not have fought for much longer. Japan would, therefore, have surrendered without the bombing of Hiroshima and Nagasaki. Sources 9 to 11 reflect this point of view.

Source 5

From an article written in 1947 by Henry Stimson, the US Secretary for War in 1945, when the bomb was dropped.

The total strength of the Japanese army was estimated at about five million men.... The air force Kamikaze, or suicide attacks...had already inflicted serious damage on our seagoing forces.... There was a very strong possibility that the Japanese government might decide upon resistance to the end.... The Allies would have been faced with the enormous task of destroying an armed force of five million men and five thousand suicide aircraft.... We estimated that if we were forced to carry this plan to its conclusion, the major fighting would not end until the latter part of 1946 at the earliest. I was informed that such operations might be expected to cost over a million casualties to American forces alone.

Source 6

Kasai Yukiko, a high school pupil in 1945, recalled in 1978 what her teacher told the class to do if the Allies invaded Japan.

When they do invade we must be ready to settle the war by drawing on our Japanese spirit and killing them. Even killing just one American soldier will do. You must be prepared to use the awls *(carpentry tools)* for self defence. You must aim for the enemy's belly. Understand? The belly! If you don't kill at least one enemy soldier, you don't deserve to live.

Source 7

This photograph shows the final second of a *kamikaze* attack on an American battleship in 1945. *Kamikaze* planes were filled with high explosive. Their pilots flew the planes into warships, committing suicide for the certainty of a direct hit. Around 5000 young Japanese volunteers died in these suicide attacks.

Source 8

Laurens van der Post, a prisoner of war in 1945, explains why he was glad the atomic bomb was dropped.

For me, selfish as it may sound, there was the certain knowledge that if the bomb had not been dropped... Field-Marshal Terauchi (*a leading Japanese commander*) would have fought on and hundreds of thousands of prisoners in his power would have been killed. Even if we had not been deliberately massacred, we were near our physical end through lack of food.

Source 9

Admiral Leahy, one of the US war leaders, wrote this in his memoirs in 1950.

The use of this barbarous weapon at Hiroshima and Nagasaki was of no material assistance in our war against Japan. The Japanese were already defeated and were ready to surrender because of the effective sea blockade and the successful bombing with conventional weapons.

Source 11

From the *Nippon Times*, a leading Japanese newspaper, on 2 August 1945.

As one step towards the solution of the food problem, the government...has made plans to collect acorns everywhere in Japan and to turn these into food. The entire people will be called upon to give their aid. School children and evacuees in particular will have to work to collect the minimum goal of 5 million koku (900,000 tonnes) of acorns.

Source 10

Saburo Hayashi, secretary to the Japanese war minister in 1945, explained in this interview in 1963 why he thought Japan could not have carried on fighting.

We thought we would be able to defeat the Americans on their first landing attempt. But if the Americans launched a second or third attack, first of all our food supply would run out. We didn't have enough weapons, nor could we have made more. Therefore if the Americans chose to come without haste the Japanese forces would have eventually had their arms up without the Americans resorting to atomic bombs.

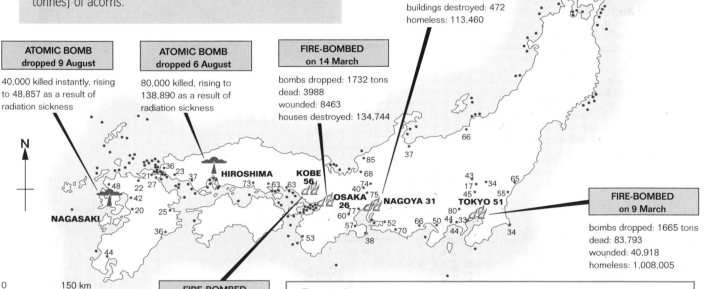

FIRE-BOMBED on 14-16 May

bombs dropped: 2515 tons
dead: 3866
buildings destroyed: 472
homeless: 113,460

ATOMIC BOMB dropped 9 August

40,000 killed instantly, rising to 48,857 as a result of radiation sickness

ATOMIC BOMB dropped 6 August

80,000 killed, rising to 138,890 as a result of radiation sickness

FIRE-BOMBED on 14 March

bombs dropped: 1732 tons
dead: 3988
wounded: 8463
houses destroyed: 134,744

FIRE-BOMBED on 9 March

bombs dropped: 1665 tons
dead: 83,793
wounded: 40,918
homeless: 1,008,005

FIRE-BOMBED on 16 March

bombs dropped: 2355 tons
dead: 2669
wounded: 11,289
homeless: 242,468

Key

 main fire-bomb attacks on major cities

• other fire-bomb attacks on towns and cities

63 numbers show percentage of buildings destroyed in each attack

atomic bomb targets

ships sunk

•

Source 12

Allied attacks on Japan in 1945.

Questions

1 Study Sources 5 to 8. According to these Sources, what might have happened in the war if the atomic bombs had not been dropped?

2 Study Sources 9 to 12. According to these Sources, what might have happened in the war if the atomic bombs had not been dropped?

3 Compare Source 5 with Source 10.

a Which writer was in favour of using the atomic bomb, and which thought it was unnecessary?

b Look at the captions for each Source to find out who these writers were. Is there anything about them which would explain why they had such different views of the same event?

c Which of the two views do you think is best supported by the information and Sources on these pages? Explain your answer.

8 The post-war world

The division of Europe

The Second World War ended in 1945. But this was not an end to change. For years to come, the changes which the war had begun continued to affect the world. One of the most crucial changes was the division of Europe by what people called 'the Iron Curtain'.

Source 1

Source 1

Allied control of Europe at the end of the Second World War, May 1945.

Source 2

The division of Europe, 1945-49.

KEY

- states which became Communist, with date of take-over
- Allied control zones: British, American, French and Soviet shown by flags
- ✠ city divided into Allied control zones
- the 'Iron Curtain'
- divisions between Allied control zones

The Allies in control of Europe

When Germany surrendered in 1945 the Allies controlled most of Europe. As Source 1 shows, twelve million Soviet troops controlled eastern Europe. Four million troops from the USA, Britain and other western Allies controlled western Europe. This gave the Allies the power to decide Europe's future.

The division of Germany

They began by splitting Germany into pieces. As Source 2 shows, the eastern part of Germany was given to Poland. The rest was divided into four zones, each occupied by an Allied army. Berlin, the capital, was also split into four sectors. Austria was separated from Germany and split into four zones.

The Allies disagree about eastern Europe

Although they agreed about Germany, the Allies disagreed about the future of eastern Europe. Stalin, the Soviet leader, wanted to keep Soviet troops there to protect his country from any future attack. But the leaders of western Europe and the USA feared that communism would spread from the Soviet Union to eastern Europe if Soviet troops stayed there. They also wanted the people of eastern Europe to choose new, democratic governments by voting in elections.

An 'iron curtain' falls across Europe

But when elections were held, the Soviet forces interfered to stop non-communists from winning. They also made sure that communists got important posts in the new governments. Winston Churchill, Britain's wartime leader, criticised these actions. He said that these events had so deeply divided eastern and western Europe that it was as if an 'iron curtain' had been drawn down between them.

A Cold War begins between East and West

The drawing down of an 'iron curtain' was only one sign of bad relations between the communist countries of the east and the non-communist countries of the west. Soon, both sides were building up their armies and stocks of weapons. Both were spying on each other and using propaganda to criticise each other. People called this hostility between them a Cold War.

The Marshall Plan

Relations between East and West grew even colder in 1947. In that year, the US President, Harry Truman, announced that the USA would give money to countries in which communists were trying to take control. The money would be used to repair war damage, such as ruined homes. He thought people would be less likely to support communists if they were well-housed and well-fed.

Seventeen countries in western Europe asked for help. Over the next three years, General Marshall of the US government gave them 13.75 billion dollars of aid. However, Stalin thought that Marshall Aid was an American plot to get more power in Europe. He would not allow the countries of eastern Europe to take Marshall Aid. As a result, the eastern countries recovered from the war more slowly than the western countries.

Source 3

This German poster of 1947 for the European Recovery Programme (ERP), better known as the Marshall Plan says 'We are building a new Europe'. In the branches of a dead tree, the countries of western Europe are growing in a nest. Doves are building the nest with Marshall Aid.

Questions

1 Look at Source 1. At the end of wars, armies usually go home. Why do you think the leaders of (a) the Soviet Union, (b) the USA and Britain did not want to bring their armies home from Europe after defeating Germany in 1945?

2 Look at Source 2.

a What was the difference between the countries on the east and the west of the 'Iron Curtain'?

b The Iron Curtain wasn't a real curtain. Why do you think Winston Churchill described the border between eastern and western Europe as one?

3 Look at Source 3.

a What do you think (i) the tree, (ii) the nest, (iii) the doves stand for?

b What does the poster suggest about (i) the ERP, (ii) the United States of America?

c Why do you think the organisers of the Marshall Plan wanted to give these messages to the German people?

The Cold War in Germany

The Cold War began in 1945 and went on until the Soviet Union collapsed in 1991. For much of that time, the Cold War was at its coldest in Germany. Why was Germany so important in this conflict between the Soviet Union and the West?

The Berlin blockade, 1948

In 1948 the Soviet Union came close to war with the West over the future of Germany. As you have read, Germany was divided into four zones. Britain, France, the USA and the Soviet Union each governed one zone. The capital, Berlin, was deep inside the Soviet zone. It too was divided into four.

Stalin wanted to keep Germany weak and divided, so that it could never threaten the Soviet Union again. But Britain, France and the USA planned to unite their zones. Stalin responded by trying to make them leave Berlin. He closed all the road, rail, and canal links through the Soviet zone to their sectors of Berlin. This blockade cut off all their food and fuel supplies.

But Britain, France and the USA refused to leave. Source 1 shows why. For the next eleven months they brought food, fuel and clothing into Berlin by air (see Source 2). The Berlin Airlift, as this was known, kept the people of West Berlin alive until Stalin ended the blockade in 1949.

Two Germanies

The Berlin blockade failed to stop the USA, Britain and France from uniting their zones. In 1949 the three zones came together to form a new country, known as West Germany. The Soviet Union replied by making its zone into a new country, known as East Germany.

The two Germanies developed in very different ways. West Germany was anti-communist and was closely linked to the USA and western Europe. Helped by Marshall Aid, it soon recovered from the war. Its economy grew so quickly that people spoke of the 'German economic miracle'. East Germany was a communist country, closely linked with the Soviet Union. Without Marshall Aid it recovered more slowly from the war. Its people were not as well off as those of West Germany.

Source 1

General Lucius Clay, commander of the American forces in Germany, explains why Western forces refused to leave West Berlin in 1948.

(If) we retreat from Berlin…Western Germany will be next…. If we withdraw our position in Berlin, Europe is threatened…. Communism will run rampant.

Source 2

Children watching American planes flying into Berlin during the Berlin Airlift. Between July 1948 and May 1949, 277,728 flights brought 1.5 million tonnes of food, fuel and other goods into the city to keep the two million people of West Berlin alive during the Berlin blockade.

Source 3

This German postcard was posted in West Berlin in 1987. It shows one of Berlin's main squares, 'Potsdamer Platz', in six different years of the twentieth century. The picture at the top shows how the Berlin Wall was built across the Square in 1961.

The Berlin Wall

When East and West Germany were created, Berlin remained a divided city inside East Germany. West Berlin belonged to West Germany, while East Berlin belonged to East Germany.

Throughout the 1950s, East Germans left their country by crossing into West Berlin. They were looking for better living conditions. By 1961 a thousand East Germans were crossing into West Berlin each day. Many were skilled workers. East Germany could not afford to lose them. On 12 and 13 August 1961, Soviet and East German workers built a high wall between East and West Berlin to stop East Germans leaving.

For the next 28 years the Berlin Wall was the most famous symbol of the Cold War. On one side were West German citizens living in a non-communist society with a good standard of living. On the other side were East German citizens living in a communist society with a poorer standard of living. Barbed wire, searchlights and watchtowers made sure that they could not escape to West Berlin.

The end of the Cold War

At the end of the 1980s the Soviet Union relaxed its control over Eastern Europe. It simply could not afford to carry on the Cold War. All over Eastern Europe, communist governments lost control. In November 1989, crossing points in the Berlin Wall were opened. Huge crowds of people quickly gathered and started to tear down the Wall. In 1990 East and West Germany were reunited as a single country.

Questions

1 Look at Source 1. Why did the British and Americans put so much effort into flying supplies into West Berlin in 1948-49?

2 Look at Source 3.
   a Describe what Potsdam Square looked like in 1929 (pictures in the bottom row).
   b How had the Square changed by 1945 (the picture in the centre row)? What caused this change?
   c What further change is shown in the picture at the top? What caused this change?
   d The postcard was made in 1987. If it were made today, what extra scene would you add to bring it up to date?

3 Sum up in a few sentences why Germany was so important in the Cold War between the Soviet Union and the West.

The United Nations

A new international body called the United Nations was set up at the end of the war. It replaced the League of Nations. What were its aims, and how was it organised to achieve them?

Origins of the United Nations

The United Nations was first thought of in a secret meeting on a ship in the Atlantic Ocean in 1941. Winston Churchill, Prime Minister of Britain, met with Roosevelt, President of the USA. The purpose of their meeting was to discuss the future of the world after the war was over. The outcome was a statement which they called The Atlantic Charter. In it, they described their 'hopes for a better world'. Their main hopes were that:

• all countries would have democratic governments
• all countries would trade freely with each other and be prosperous
• all countries would reduce their weapons.

Several months later, Roosevelt suggested that all the Allied countries at war should be called The United Nations. Twenty-six countries agreed with this suggestion and signed a United Nations Declaration, saying that they agreed with the Atlantic Charter. Over the next three years, their numbers grew as more countries joined the Allies. By 1945 there were fifty of them.

The United Nations Charter

Representatives of the fifty countries met in San Francisco in April 1945. They set up a new world body to put the Atlantic Charter into effect. They called it the United Nations Organisation (UN), and set out its aims in a document called the Charter. Source 2 shows the main aims of the Charter.

Source 1

An Allied poster of 1942 shows the flags of the countries which signed the United Nations Declaration at the start of that year.

Source 2

From the Charter of the United Nations, September 1945.

The purposes of the United Nations are:

1   to maintain international peace and security...
2   to develop friendly relations among nations...
3   to achieve international co-operation in solving international problems ... and in encouraging respect for human rights and for fundamental freedoms without distinction as to race, sex, language or religion, and
4   to be a centre for harmonising the actions of nations in the attainment of those common ends.

The structure of the United Nations

In January 1946, a UN General Assembly met in London. This was a sort of world parliament, with representatives from every member country. It set up the organisations shown in Source 3. The most important of these was the Security Council. Then it decided that the UN's permanent headquarters should be in New York. In 1952 the UN moved into the specially built headquarters shown in the picture.

The General Assembly

A sort of world parliament. Each country has one vote. It discusses all kinds of world problems and suggests solutions.

Secretariat

The staff of the UN, led by a Secretary-General. They do the day-to-day work of the UN, e.g. interpreters, translators, secretaries, clerks.

The International Court of Justice

Based at The Hague in Holland. It has fifteen judges from different countries. It judges legal disputes between countries.

The Security Council

A decision-making body with five permanent members (Britain, France, USA, USSR, China) and six (now ten) members chosen by the Assembly. It meets whenever there is a dispute between members. It can try to stop one country attacking another by:

- asking all members of the UN not to trade with that country
- ordering a ceasefire
- sending UN observers to check that UN orders have been obeyed
- sending armed troops to enforce a ceasefire.

Decisions need a 'yes' vote from all five permanent members.

The Trusteeship Council

Supervises the progress of some former colonies towards independence. (Only a few small islands in the Pacific were still colonies in 1995.)

The Economic and Social Council

27 member countries elected by the General Assembly co-ordinate the social and economic work of the UN through 52 commissions, agencies, committees and special bodies. The 'Big Four' agencies are:

The International Labour Organisation which tries to improve workers' rights, conditions, wages and insurance throughout the world.

The World Health Organisation which co-ordinates medical research, monitors infectious diseases, mounts health campaigns, does research, etc.

UN Educational, Scientific and Cultural Organisation which helps nations to co-operate through education, science and culture.

Food and Agriculture Organisation which works to raise nutrition levels, and to improve the production and distribution of food.

Source 3

The United Nations Headquarters in New York, photographed from a plane flying above the East River, nears completion in 1952.

Questions

1 a Look at Source 1. What was this poster meant to make people think about the United Nations?
   b How did it create this impression?

2 Read Source 2.
   a How long after Source 1 was the Charter written?
   b Do the purposes of the UN in the Charter seem different from the purposes shown in the poster?

3 Look at Source 3 and then look back to Source 2 on page 41. In what ways was the UN (a) similar to, (b) different from the League of Nations?

Recovery from the war

As soon as the war was over, people began to repair the damage to their countries. Some countries, including those which had been defeated, recovered quickly. Others, including Britain, recovered slowly. Why was this so?

How Japan recovered

Japan in 1945 was in ruins. Two million people were dead. Four buildings in every ten had been destroyed by bombs. There was no oil. Most of the country's ships had been sunk. Millions faced starvation.

Three things helped the Japanese to recover from all this.

- The Americans gave Japan huge amounts of money. They were thinking of the future and wanted a properous country to trade with. Over the next five years they poured two billion dollars of aid into Japan.
- The government took land from landowners and sold it to peasants at low prices. Now that they had land of their own, the peasants worked harder and grew more food than before. And the more they earned from selling food, the more they spent in the shops. This helped factories which made shop goods.
- The Japanese worked very hard. They were also ready to accept low wages. Employers could therefore spend their profits on buying new machinery instead of on pay rises.

Source 1

The main street of Hiroshima in 1952.

How Germany recovered

In the British, French and American zones of Germany, the Allied forces quickly organised a massive rebuilding programme. Every able-bodied person was made to do building work. But in the Soviet zone, rebuilding was much slower. The Soviet Union had been badly damaged in the war. The Soviets were more interested in repairing their own damage. They took huge amounts of machinery and raw materials from their zone of Germany to help do this.

As you have read (page 92), the British, Americans and French decided to make their zones into one. They wanted to spend as little as possible on occupying Germany. They also wanted Germany to recover quickly so that it could trade with other countries and help them to recover too. With their backing, and with Marshall Aid (see page 91), West Germany soon became the fastest growing economy in Europe. East Germany, under Soviet influence, lagged far behind.

This photograph, from *Life* magazine in 1951, shows a typical American family with the amount of food an average American family ate in a year.

How the Allies recovered

Britain and the United States recovered from the war in very different ways. The United States recovered quickest. No part of the USA had been bombed or occupied, so there was no war damage to repair. This meant that factories could quickly switch from making war materials to consumer goods such as cars and household equipment. Millions of workers started buying such things with money they had earned and saved during the war. This led to an economic boom which made many Americans rich (see Source 2).

Britain in 1945 was in bad shape. It was the only Allied country which had fought from the very start to the end of the war. Factories, docks, mines, railways and roads were worn out. The government owed £3 billion to other countries. The only way Britain could recover was to earn more money by selling things to other countries - machinery or cars, for example. This also meant buying fewer things from abroad. One result of this was that the British people went through a period of 'austerity' in which they had to do without many things. Some things were rationed even more strictly than in wartime. Coal and other fuels were scarce. Housing was in short supply. The scene shown in Source 3 is typical of Britain in the postwar years.

Questions

1 Compare Source 1 with the picture of Hiroshima on page 86 (Source 3).

  a How many years passed between the taking of these two photographs?

  b Judging by these photographs, how did the city change during that time?

  c How can those changes be explained?

2 Look at Sources 2 and 3.

  a What do these pictures tell you about Britain and the USA in the five years after the war?

  b How can the differences between the two be explained?

A queue outside a butcher's shop in London in 1947.

War and the Welfare State

· ·

During the war, the British government made plans to provide health care, schooling, insurance benefits and housing on a far bigger scale than before. Why did it make these plans in a time of war, and how were these plans put into effect?

Source 1

From *Town People Through Country Eyes*, a survey of evacuated children collected by 1700 Women's Institutes all over Britain in 1941.

Some children (from Manchester) had never slept in beds.... One boy (from Salford) had never had a bath before.... The state of the children (from Liverpool) was such that the school had to be fumigated after reception....

Bread and lard are a usual breakfast for a number of (Walthamstow) children when at home.... Few Manchester children would eat food that demanded the use of teeth - they could only eat with a teaspoon.... One little girl of five (from Liverpool) remarked that she would like to have beer and cheese for supper.... Some (Gosport) children had never used a knife and fork. The (Finsbury) children did not understand sitting down for a meal but seemed to like food in the hand.

The war changes public opinion

The war changed the way in which people thought about their society. Public opinion surveys showed that most people hoped for a fairer, better society after the war was over. There were three reasons for this new mood:

- The war opened many people's eyes to the poverty of Britain's cities. Many of the 1.5 million women and children evacuated in 1939 were from poor families. Source 1 describes the condition of some of the children.

- The war brought people together. Millions of men and women shared experiences such as evacuation, rationing, and air-raids. This broke down barriers and made people feel they were fighting in a common cause.

- The war forced the government to involve itself more closely in health and social services. For example, to make sure that food rationing did not harm children's health, the government provided all children with free school milk, orange juice, cod-liver oil, and vitamin tablets.

Planning a new society

A huge number of plans for a fairer society were drawn up during the war. The most famous plan was called Social Insurance and Allied Services. Its author, Sir William Beveridge, suggested that people should pay weekly contributions to a government-run insurance scheme. This would give them help if they could not help themselves - if, for example, they were out of work, sick or disabled. At the same time, the government would provide family allowances, improve health services, and maintain full employment.

The Beveridge Plan was an instant bestseller. One hundred thousand copies were sold when it came out in December 1942. It was so popular that the government was forced to set up a Reconstruction Committee to plan Britain's future after the war. This committee drew up detailed plans for major changes in education, health, housing, insurance and employment.

Labour wins the 1945 election

Soon after the war ended in 1945, a general election was held. In the election campaign, the Labour Party promised that it would put the new plans into effect without delay. But the Conservative leader, Winston Churchill, warned voters that Britain was very poor. He said that putting the plans into effect quickly would be hard. The election result was a landslide victory for Labour. This was partly because most of the soldiers who voted chose Labour. Source 2 suggests one reason why they did this.

The welfare state is born

The new Labour government quickly carried out its election promises. It introduced the following:

- National Insurance. All workers had to pay for a weekly insurance stamp costing 25p. Their employers and the government also paid contributions towards the stamp. These stamps were stuck on a card. Having a paid-up card entitled the holder to unemployment or sickness pay, retirement and widow's pension, maternity benefits, and a funeral allowance.
- National Assistance. People not in paid work who did not have a card - for example, disabled people - could get help from a National Assistance Board.
- The National Health Service. All medical treatment was to be free for everybody. Local authorities had to provide medical services such as ambulances, midwives and immunisation.

This combination of National Insurance, National Assistance and a National Health Service made Britain into what people called a 'welfare state' - a country in which the government takes a high level of responsibility for the health and welfare of its citizens.

Source 2

This poster was made by the Army Bureau of Current Affairs in 1944. It shows a child with rickets (a disease caused by poor nutrition) in the ruins of a bombed-out Britain. The new health centre in front suggests what postwar Britain could be like. Winston Churchill, the Prime Minister, banned this poster soon after it appeared.

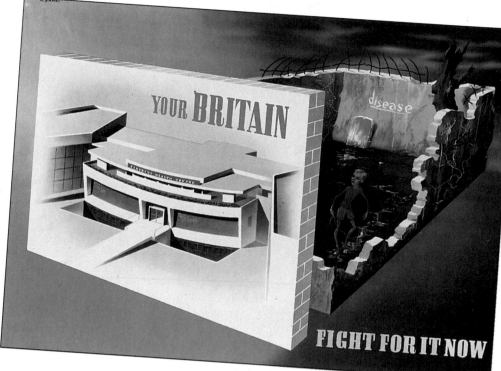

YOUR BRITAIN

disease

FIGHT FOR IT NOW

Questions

1. a What impression does Source 1 give of evacuated children?
   b How might this have made some people think that British society needed to change?

2. Look at Source 2.
   a This poster was suggesting that Britain would change if people fought and won the war. What kind of change does the poster suggest would take place?
   b Why might people in 1944 have agreed with the message of the poster?
   c Why might Winston Churchill have decided to ban it?

3. a In your own words, explain what the term 'welfare state' means.
   b Give as many reasons as you can why Britain became a welfare state so soon after the war.

Depth Study

9 War and the end of the Indian empire

At the start of this century, Britain ruled some 450 million people living in fifty-six colonies and dominions all over the world. Together, they made up the British Empire. It was the biggest empire the world had ever known.

Fifty years later, after two world wars, the British Empire was breaking apart. One by one, its colonies became independent countries. Today, near the end of the century, all that remains of this mighty empire are a few tiny islands.

The end of the British Empire was one of the most important changes of the twentieth century. Part 9 of this book shows how and why it happened in the most valuable part of the Empire - India. We begin by finding out what India was like in the early years of the century.

Source 1

This Victorian map shows the British Empire near the start of the twentieth century. Britain's possessions are shown in red. Some of the peoples of the Empire are shown at the top and bottom.

India before the wars

The country and its people

India was one of Britains's largest possessions. It was larger than Europe, and fifteen times bigger than the British Isles. About 300 million people lived there.

These people were divided in many ways. They spoke fifteen main languages, such as Hindi and Punjabi in the north and centre, Urdu and Gujarati in the west, Bengali in the east, and Tamil in the south. Each language was written in its own script, and spoken in many dialects.

Above all, the Indians were divided by religion. There were 207 million Hindus, 62.5 million Muslims, 6 million Sikhs, and millions of Buddhists, Christians and members of sects. On many occasions in the past there had been fighting and hatred between different religious groups, especially Hindus and Muslims.

Source 2

This photograph was taken in Delhi in 1903. It shows a Durbar, or ceremonial gathering, of the most important people in India. The Viceroy of India, Lord Curzon, and his wife are sitting in a gold-embossed *howdah* on the elephant on the left. On the right, Indian princes are carried past on elephants decorated with fine cloth, gold, silver, diamonds and pearls.

The government of India

About two thirds of India were governed by the British. The head of the government was the British monarch. He or she was represented in India by a Viceroy, based in the capital, Delhi. Under the Viceroy's command were Governors, each ruling a province. Some 70,000 British soldiers and civil servants did the day-to-day work of running these provinces.

The other third of India was made up of 601 princely states. Each was governed by an Indian prince - a Rajah or Maharajah in Hindu states, and a Nizam or Nawab in Muslim states. They ruled their states by themselves, but they had to allow British advisers to help them. The British thus had a hand in ruling the princely states.

To do

Ask your teacher for Copymaster 34. Use it as the basis for a wall display or illustrated talk about India at the start of the century. Use the information on these pages, as well as any other information you can find in the library to add to it.

What did Indian people think about the British ruling their country? And what did the British themselves think about it? The sources on these two pages show a range of their views.

Some British views of British rule

Most British people were proud of their rule in India. They called it 'the Raj', an Indian word meaning rule, or dominion. They said that India was 'the jewel in the Crown' of the British Empire.

One reason for such pride was their record of achievement. By 1900 the British had built 80,000 km of railways throughout India. They had made dams and dug over 100,000 km of canals for irrigation and transport. They had brought law and order. Above all, they had brought peace between states which had often made war on each other in the past. Sources 3 and 4 show how some British officials saw themselves and their work.

Source 3

This dinner menu was decorated with pictures by a British official in the Indian Civil Service in 1904. The pictures show various aspects of the work of the Indian Civil Service.

Source 4

From a speech by Lord Curzon, a former Viceroy of India, in 1907.

Wherever this Empire has extended its borders, misery and oppression, lawlessness and poverty ... have been replaced by peace, justice, prosperity, humanity and freedom.

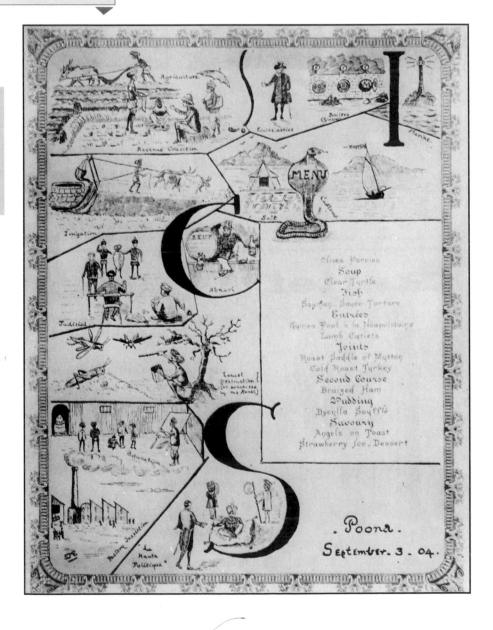

Some Indian views of British rule

Most Indians probably had no views about the British. They were too busy scraping a living from the land. Many others, such as those who worked for the British may have welcomed British rule. But some saw British rule as unfair. Source 5 shows some of the reasons why.

Since 1885, an Indian National Congress had been pressing for more equality for Indians. They also demanded the right to govern themselves (see Source 6). As you might guess from Source 6, members of the Congress were educated, middle class people. They used peaceful methods to put across their point of view. But, as Source 7 shows, some Indians saw violence as the way to oppose British rule.

Source 7

This is an advertisement for the *Kali* brand of cigarettes, printed in 1908. It contains a hidden message. It shows the Hindu goddess Kali as a bloodthirsty killer, trampling on the body of her lover, Shiva, and cutting off the heads of British as well as Indian people. The writing urges people to buy Kali cigarettes 'to look after the interests of this country's poor and humble workers'.

Source 5

From a leaflet written by Indians in Bengal in 1907.

Who Governs Us?
Can these thieves really be our rulers? These thieves ... import a huge number of goods, made in their own country, and sell them in our markets, stealing our wealth and taking life from our people. Can those who steal the harvest of our fields and doom us to hunger, fever and plague, really be our rulers? Can foreigners really be our rulers, foreigners who impose on us ever more taxes?

Source 6

From a speech made in 1897 by a member of the Indian National Congress.

From our earliest schooldays the great English writers have been our classics. Englishmen have been our teachers .... English history is taught in our schools .... It is impossible not to ... acquire English ideas of duty, of rights, of brotherhood .... Filled with these ideas and principles, we naturally want to have the full rights and to share the responsibilities of British citizenship.

Questions

1 Look at Source 3.
  a What do the pictures on the menu tell you about the work that the Indian Civil Service was doing in 1904?
  b Judging by the pictures, what did the civil servant who drew them think about the work of the Indian Civil Service? Explain your answer.

2 Read Sources 4 and 5.
  a Which Source is in favour of British rule and which is against it?
  b How can the differences in view be explained?

3 Judging by Sources 5 and 6, why did some Indians want to govern themselves instead of being ruled by the British?

4 Source 7 is an advertisement for cigarettes, but it doesn't only tell us about cigarettes. How can it be used to tell us about the way some Indians felt about (a) religion, (b) British rule, in 1908?

India after the First World War

The Indians who wanted an end to British rule made little progress before 1914. The British simply ignored their demands. After the First World War they started to give the Indians some say in how India was governed. But this did not satisfy them. Why did this happen after the war? And why did it not satisfy the Indians?

India in the First World War

India played a major part in the First World War. Some 800,000 Indian soldiers fought on Britain's side in Europe and the Middle East. India also gave Britain huge amounts of money, food and materials. As a result, taxes rose, prices increased, and there were shortages of food and fuel. Many Indians felt they should be rewarded for this contribution to Britain's war effort. They supported demands by the Indian National Congress for self-government.

These feelings grew stronger at the end of the war. The peacemakers (see page 26) gave many European people the right to rule themselves. Indians asked why they too should not have this right.

Source 1

The writing on this poster says:
This soldier is protecting his home and family. The best way to help your family and countrymen is by joining the army.

यह सिपाही हिन्दुस्तान की हिफ़ाज़त कर रहा है । वह अपने घर और घरवारवालों की हिफ़ाज़त कर रहा है ॥
अपने घरवारवालों की मद्द करने का सब से अच्छा तरीक़ा यह है कि फ़ौज में भरती हो जाओ ॥

The Government of India Act

In 1919 the British responded to these demands. They made a Government of India Act, changing the way India was governed. It gave the vote to about five million Indians, mostly wealthy people. It set up law-making councils in each province and gave Indians more seats in them than the British. It also said that the ministers who controlled education and public health in the provinces could be Indian.

Some members of Congress welcomed these changes. Others were bitterly disappointed. India would still be governed by the Viceroy and the Indian Civil Service. And the ministers who controlled taxation, the police and the law courts in the provinces would all still be British.

Massacre at Amritsar

At the same time as making these changes, the British made laws to deal with people who opposed their rule. The laws gave the British the right to imprison opponents without trial. This angered Congress. It organised protests against the new laws.

The leader of these protests was a lawyer called Mohandas Gandhi. He encouraged people to go on strike and to make peaceful protests with prayers and fasting. In some places, however, the protests turned into riots. In the province of Punjab, the local army commander, General Dyer, banned all protest meetings. But in the town of Amritsar, people ignored the ban. On 13 April 1919, thousands of protesters gathered for a mass meeting. General Dyer decided to break up the meeting by force. On his orders, British soldiers fired into the crowd, killing 379 men, women and children.

Congress rejects the reforms

The massacre at Amritsar was a turning point. Indians everywhere were horrified by the killings. Dyer's name became a term of abuse. Gandhi compared the British with Satan and said that they could not be trusted. He persuaded Congress to reject the changes made by the Government of India Act. Instead, Congress decided to work for self-rule for India as quickly as possible.

Source 2

A citizen of Amritsar points to a bullet hole in the square where British soldiers shot dead 379 people on 13 April 1919. Chalked on the wall is graffiti about General Dyer, who gave the order to shoot.

Questions

1
  a How was India affected by the First World War?
  b Why did India's involvement in the war make Indians want an end to British rule even more than they had wanted it before?
  c Why do you think the British changed the way they governed India in 1919?

2
  a What powers did the Government of India Act give to Indian people?
  b Why do you think some members of Congress were pleased by the Act?
  c Why were others disappointed by it?

3
  Look at Source 2. Suggest (politely!) what kinds of things the graffiti might have said about General Dyer.

Campaigns for self-rule

What methods did Indian people use in their bid to get self-rule after the First World War? And how successful were they?

Gandhi and the Congress Party

The best known Indian working to free India from British rule was Mohandas Gandhi. His picture (Source 1) tells us a lot about him. He wore only a loin-cloth, and span cotton on a spinning wheel every day, to encourage people to live simple, truthful lives. It was also a way of telling them to be proud of their way of life, and to reject British customs and methods.

Gandhi told Indians to oppose the British with what he called 'truth force' (*satyagraha* in Hindi). This meant that they should do all they could to make life difficult for the British, but never use violence. The methods he suggested included strikes, demonstrations, and boycotts (for example, refusing to buy British-made goods). Under Gandhi's leadership, these became the main ways in which Congress campaigned for self-rule.

Gandhi's most famous protest is shown in Source 2. In 1930 he led thousands of Indians to the Indian coast. There they made salt from sea-water. This was against the law. Only government-approved companies were allowed to make salt in India, because the British raised large amounts of money by taxing salt. As the news spread of what Gandhi was doing, many thousands of people all over India started making their own salt. Gandhi was arrested. By the middle of the year, over 100,000 campaigners were in prison.

Gandhi asked people to protest peacefully against the British. But all too often, protests turned into violence. Peaceful marches turned into riots. Policemen were murdered. Often, the violence was in revenge for harsh treatment by the British forces in India (see Source 3).

Source 1

This photograph, taken in 1925, shows Mohandas Gandhi sitting cross-legged by the wheel on which he span cotton every day.

Source 2

In this picture, Gandhi (background left) and his supporters are breaking the law by picking up salt from the sea-shore in 1930.

Jinnah and the Muslim League

The leaders of Congress said that Congress was a national party, standing for Indians of all kinds (see Source 4). Muslims disagreed. They thought that Congress favoured Hindus. They gave their support to a party called the Muslim League, led by Mohammed Ali Jinnah.

Like Congress, the Muslim League wanted an end to British rule. But, unlike Congress, it wanted to split India into two countries, one made from the areas where most people were Muslims. They named this country after those areas: P for Punjab, A for Afghania, K for Kashmir, S for Sind, and TAN for Baluchistan. The word that this made, PAKISTAN, means 'Land of the Pure' in Urdu.

Source 3

This calendar commemorates Baghat Singh who shot a British policeman in revenge for the police killing of a Congress leader in 1931. He was hanged (centre) for this. The artist has painted him with a traditional warrior's moustache to suggest bravery.

Source 4

This Congress Party poster was made in 1931. It shows Hindus, Muslims and others walking along the 'path of liberty' to a mountain top where Mother India is sitting. However, a broken bridge is preventing the walkers from reaching her. Their leaders have fallen through the bridge into a prison. Some have been swept away in the river. Mother India is talking to the Hindu god Krishna, who says 'with a little more sacrifice the road will be complete'.

The Government of India Act, 1935

Neither peaceful campaigns nor violent protests won self-rule for India between the wars. However, some progress was made. In 1935 the British made another Government of India Act. This set up elected parliaments in eleven provinces. These had the power to make laws for the provinces. In the elections which followed, Congress won in nine provinces. Thus it gained the power to make laws in much of India. India, however, was still part of the British Empire, ruled by a Viceroy.

Questions

1 Look at Source 2.
  a Why was there a law against what these people were doing?
  b If all Indians had started getting salt in this way, how would this have affected the British in India?
  c How does this help to explain why (i) Gandhi organised this protest, (ii) the British used great violence against the protesters?

2 a What does Source 4 tell us about the Congress Party's campaign to end British rule in India?
  b Suggest why the Congress leaders are shown in prison.
  c What might an Indian Muslim have said about this poster in 1931?

India in the Second World War

In 1939, when the Second World War began, India still did not have self-rule. Exactly two years after the war ended, the British left India. What happened during the war to help India get self-rule?

> There was something rotten when one man, a foreigner..., could plunge 400 million human beings into war without the slightest reference to them.

India goes to war

Although Congress now controlled many of India's provinces, the British Viceroy still ruled India. On 3 September, without consulting Congress, he declared that India was at war with Germany. As Source 1 shows, this angered the Congress leaders. But there was nothing they could do about it. Over the next five years, 2.5 million Indians joined the armed forces, fighting in Europe, Africa and the Far East.

India was important to both sides in the war. Britain had to fight not only in Europe but also in Africa and Asia. It could not do so without help from its colonies and dominions (see Source 2). Japan wanted to build up its own empire in Asia and the Pacific. It could not do so while Britain still controlled India. As well as trying to invade India, the Japanese therefore encouraged Indians to rebel against British rule (see Source 3).

Quit India

Faced with this threat from Japan, the British needed to make sure that India stayed loyal to them. To get the support of Congress, they promised that India could become a dominion, like Australia or Canada, after the war. But Gandhi and Congress wanted full independence without delay. They began a 'Quit India' campaign to persuade the British to leave immediately.

The Quit India campaign brought India close to revolution. When the leaders of Congress were arrested, strikes and demonstrations swept the country. Thousands were killed and injured in riots. Over 100,000 were arrested.

TOGETHER

Source 3

This poster was dropped on India by Japanese planes in 1942. It shows Indians working as servants for a British officer. Servants in the background are rebelling against another British officer. The writing, in Hindi and Bengali, says '...Why must Indians stay slaves? Seize this chance - rise!'

The war weakens British rule

The British managed to crush the Quit India campaign, but their hold on India was weakened in other ways. As the war went on, more and more Indians got senior jobs in the army and civil service. This gave them experience in running their own affairs, and gave them more self-confidence.

British rule was also weakened by events outside India. In 1941, for example, the leaders of Britain and the USA signed the Atlantic Charter (see page 94). In it, they described their 'hopes for a better future of the world'. One of their hopes was that all countries should have democratic governments (see Source 4). This raised the hopes of people all over the world that they would become self-governing after the war.

The Labour government of 1945

Soon after the war ended, British voters elected a Labour government. It decided to give India self-rule as quickly as possible. This was partly because Labour had been sympathetic to the idea of Indian self-rule for many years. Partly too it was because it wanted to concentrate on rebuilding Britain after the war.

Source 4

One of the hopes for a better future in the *Atlantic Charter* signed by Churchill and Roosevelt in 1941.

3 They respect the right of all peoples to choose the form of government under which they will live ....

Questions

1 Read Source 1. Why were the leaders of Congress angry when the Viceroy took India to war in 1939?

2 Look at Source 2. Why was it important for Britain to have these soldiers 'Together'?

3 Look at Source 3.
   a How does the poster suggest that Indians were slaves?
   b In what other way, not shown in the poster, might Indians have felt they were slaves?
   c Explain which of the two posters (Sources 2 and 3) you think members of Congress would most have agreed with during the war.

4 a Read Source 4. How might this have weakened Britain's rule in India?
   b What other developments during the war helped to weaken Britain's rule in India?

The break-up of British India

On 15 August 1947, India became free of British rule. Millions of Indians had dreamed of this for years. Yet, within days, India was swept by massacres in which at least 200,000 people died. Why did British rule end in such appalling violence?

Source 1

From an interview with Mohammed Ali Jinnah in 1944.

How can you even dream of Hindu-Muslim unity? Everything pulls us apart. We have no inter-marriages. We have not the same calendar. The Muslims believe in a single God, and the Hindus worship idols .... The Hindus worship animals. They consider cows sacred. We, the Muslims, think it is nonsense. We want to kill the cows. We want to eat them ....There are only two links between the Muslims and the Hindus: British rule - and the common desire to get rid of it.

Source 2

An eye-witness of the Calcutta massacres describes what he saw from a boat in the Hooghly river.

People with their hands tied were brought to the river's edge and then pushed down the bank into the water, where men in dinghies prodded them under with poles. Others were being laid on their faces, with their heads poking out over the Howrah bridge and being beheaded into the river, their bodies thrown in afterwards. After the riot the river was literally choked with dead bodies.

Congress and the Muslim League

As you have read, India's two main parties, Congress and the Muslim League, had different ideas about self-rule. Congress wanted India to be one country with one government that stood for all religions. The Muslim League wanted a separate country for Muslims. Source 1 shows why Jinnah, the Muslim leader, felt that this was needed.

The British began talks about independence with the two parties in 1946. But Congress and the League remained divided on the issue of a united India. The talks broke down.

The breakdown of Hindu-Muslim relations

While the politicians argued, ordinary people were taking matters into their own hands. In many places, relations between Hindus and Muslims had been bad for a long time. Now they started to break down completely. The worst breakdown happened in Calcutta. A peaceful demonstration by Muslims against both Congress and the British turned into a riot, and then into a massacre (see Source 2). 4,000 people were killed and 100,000 lost their homes. Many fled from the city and became refugees (see Source 3).

Source 3

This Hindu family was photographed leaving Bengal in autumn 1946, after riots spread from Calcutta to the rest of the region.

The partition of India

The violence in India convinced the British that they must hand over power quickly. In 1947 a new Viceroy, Lord Mountbatten, was sent to India to arrange this. Faced with growing bloodshed, Mountbatten soon decided that India must be split into two countries - India and Pakistan (see Source 4). The Princely States would choose whether they wanted to belong to India or Pakistan.

Independence and massacres

British rule ended on 15 August 1947. On that day, India and Pakistan came into being. However, it had been impossible to draw the borders so that all Hindus were in India and all Muslims were in Pakistan. Millions of Hindus and Muslims now found themselves in the 'wrong' country. There were also millions of Sikhs in the Punjab, who felt they belonged to neither. Almost immediately, these groups came under attack. Soon, 14 million people had left their homes, fleeing for safety to the other side of the border. Many did not make it. Whole groups of refugees were massacred as they went (see Source 5). Nobody knows how many died in these massacres. The lowest estimate made by historians is 200,000. It may have been half a million.

Source 5

How India was partitioned in August 1947. Areas where more than half the people were Muslim (shown in yellow) became Pakistan. Areas where more than half were Hindu (shown in brown) became India. But in the Muslim areas there were many Hindus (shown with brown dots), and in Hindu areas where there were many Muslims (yellow dots), it was impossible to draw borders between the two religions.

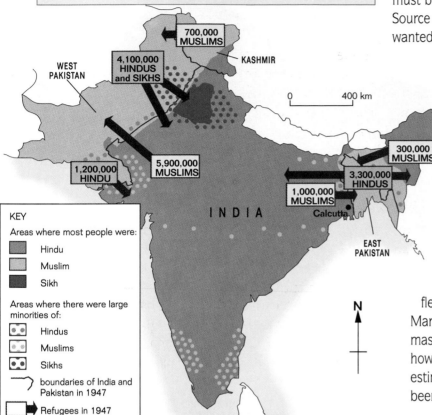

KEY

Areas where most people were:

- Hindu
- Muslim
- Sikh

Areas where there were large minorities of:

- Hindus
- Muslims
- Sikhs

boundaries of India and Pakistan in 1947

Refugees in 1947

Source 5

A motor lorry laden with Sikh-Hindu refugees passes the military check point on the Pakistan – India border on the road between Amritsar, India and Lahore, Pakistan.

Questions

1 Read Source 1. Explain in your own words why Jinnah thought that unity between Hindus and Muslims was impossible.

2 Look carefully at Source 3.

a Make a list of all the women's possessions you can see in the picture.

b What does each possession tell you about what they were doing?

c How does Source 2 help to explain why they were doing this?

3 Look at Source 4.

a Why was it impossible to draw the new borders so that all Hindus were included in India and all Muslims were included in Pakistan?

b What do you think Sikh people disliked about the new borders?

4 Look at Source 5. Using all the sources and information on these pages, suggest why these people did not want to remain in their homes.

Index